Also by Daniel Brand

Outlaws of the Wild West

Infamous Western Criminals and Killers

Daniel Brand

Introduction

"I want results when I fight."

- Frank James

The fight for life, to achieve greatness, and become all one desires is one thing that's common to all mankind. That fight is also one of the building blocks of America's history. America's history is replete with people whose life challenges have helped to shape their final outcomes. Their experiences, in the long run, sometimes eventually help shape life for other members of society. These are some of the issues that shaped most of the characters that make up the outlaws of the Wild West.

When you think of the Wild West or Outlaws of the Wild West, the picture that comes to mind is usually a gory one. You may think of violence, murders, bank robberies, train robberies, and all sorts of other unpleasant occurrences. As for the personalities, you may think about gunslingers, the prospectors, cowboys, gunfighters, gangs, gamblers, or outlaws. All these personalities and activities form a part of what the wild West represented. But that's not all there is to see in some of the outlaws of the wild West. You should ask yourself, what influenced the lives and actions of these outlaws? What characterized their life's journey? How did they start? How did they get to their current state?

The famous Wild West era represents the period immediately after the American Civil War. It spans from around 1865 to late 1895, with the frontier officially coming to an end. However, some experts extend the era into the early parts of the 1920s. You can also refer to the Wild West as the American

Frontier. It covers the western side of the Mississippi River to include areas like Arizona, California, Colorado, Dakota, Idaho, Montana, Oregon, Nevada, and New Mexico.

Post civil war life in the Wild West was not an easy one. This era marked a period of survival. Promoters and proprietors would do anything to survive or keep their agricultural or mining activities afloat. Business owners wanted to get labor at ridiculously low rates, including more hours from employees with no pay for extra hours. Workers formed unions to press home their demands and get more value for their time. Due to extensive travels, quite a notable number of proprietors were Irish or German migrants.

Rival groups or gangs emerged in a bid to ensure business interests within the county, and so it remains protected. The local authority or sheriff would usually get overwhelmed with the demand for justice. A situation where just a handful of persons, say three or four, have the responsibility to maintain law and order in a city of over two thousand makes it necessary for private militia and security for businesses. Raids of farmlands and cattle were some of the common issues to deal with. These and more made the Wild West a notorious place to live.

One of the critical policies of President Grover Cleveland (America's 22nd and 24th president, from 1885 to 1889 and 1893 and 1897, respectively) was bringing an end to the events of the Wild West.

Popular outlaws and cowboys in the Old West include the likes of Billy the Kid, John Wesley Hardin, Ben Johnson, Annie Oakley, Will Rogers, Doc Scurlock, Cliven Bundy, Ty Murray, and more. However, this book takes a look at some of the not-so-famous outlaws in the Wild West. There are interesting facts and tales not explored about these outlaws and their anecdotes that make them a must-read. Some outlaws of the Old West are young men in their prime, teenage and early twenties. These men were faced with surviving in a harsh environment with extreme weather and little or no support. Some of them have better parental backgrounds and opportunities but got caught in the web of deceit, violence, and the need to survive.

However, if you take a more in-depth look at some of the characters that make up the Wild West, you would discover men with a fighting spirit, the will to survive against all the odds. Some other outlaws ironically had the zeal to see justice served and more. As hard as it might sound, some of the outlaws of the Wild West were men whose circumstances created the worst out of them. Today, you can read about their life story and decide for yourself if these men were really outlaws or victims of an evolving system.

This book, the Outlaws of the Wild West, strives to present you with an unusual read, inspiring, insightful, and informative. My overall intent for writing this book is not entertainment alone, but to model the themes of bravery, skill, resilience, and the ability to rise above all odds to achieve your goals.

If you wonder why I chose to pick examples of inspiring characters and role models from outlaws, then I ask you, if roses could have thorns, why not outlaws of the Wild West? There is always something positive to pick from any story or incident.

At the end of this book, you should have a better grasp of what life in the Wild West looked like, the outlaws, and what makes their stories unique. You should also be able to see yourself play out in each of the characters. Look out for your weaknesses and watch your strengths play out in these characters. See how best to harness your power and overcome your weaknesses.

When you finish reading this book, you should have a clearer picture of the events that unfolded in the Wild West, be inspired to take on more positive roles in a society evolving for better, and have a good sense of mind to follow your dreams.

About the Author: **Daniel Brand**

Daniel Brand not only follows American history but loves to live the American dream. Growing up in Kansas and seeing the classics of western America, Daniel dreamt of being a cowboy, as most young boys do. At an early age of 4, little Daniel looked forward to the times when he would run wild on the prairies of his home.

He, however, grew up to realize that it could only be a dream and not a reality. The West, as it was known then, was no longer in existence. Daniel, therefore, channeled his love for the West by digging deep into the history of the westerners, their culture, lives, challenges, and victories. The outlaws became one of Daniel's newest pursuits. Thus, he compiled a list and delved into the life and times of some of the fascinating criminals of the Wild West. He tells their story in a new way to inspire greatness in the American people.

Chapter One: Was the West Really So Wild?

It's 1862, and John Joshua, like every other young man, made the long journey on horseback to the West. With limited means of survival or skill, he saw the West as the best place to start a new life and to fend for himself. But, there were tales of how wild things could get in the West—that sort of scared him a bit. The thought of trying his luck elsewhere crossed his mind, but with not much to lose, he, along with his friend Collins Rudolph, saw no harm in giving the West a shot.

The journey to the West was usually an arduous one. One had to traverse the wilderness roads, rough and steep terrain, with frequent extreme weather conditions. Travelers would occasionally come across bandits and more on such territories. If you were lucky or in the company of well-armed personnel, then you would get away without a scratch. At other times, you could end up losing your wares and other personal belongings. This was the journey John and Collins embarked on to make it to the Wild West in search of greener pastures.

Along the line, John and Collins went by several mines and rail routes with workers trying to erk a living. They sometimes stayed behind to carry out menial jobs for a few days before continuing their journey. Usually, people moved in droves when traveling to the frontier. You would see dozens of wagons stretching out several kilometers with a massive cloud of dust. The roads were mostly narrow; therefore, it was almost impossible to beat the traffic. At most, two mid-sized wagons could travel side by side. It was usually a nightmare traveling those routes to the Wild West.

You would need a pair of goggles to travel to make the trip. This, however, was a luxury John and Collins would not enjoy. Like other poor folks, they made the long trip from their respective countries across Europe to the West. The only option left for some of these folks was to look like a fresh cloud of walking earth.

Fortunately for the duo, their journey paid off as they safely landed in New Mexico unhurt and with their small belongings intact. When they walked in, they made a stop at a local inn just to get something to eat and drink before deciding on what to do next.

John played out one of the scenes he saw on their way in. They had passed by a ranch with an entire family hard at work, taking care of their ranch. The man of the house and his sons worked hard at milking the cattle. John and Collins were fortunate to get casual work at the Woodpecker's family ranch in exchange for two nights of shelter and food while staying with the family. He would recall how difficult the life of a cowboy really would be.

How Truly Wild did the West Go?

The need for survival could cause things to heat up quickly, especially in a post-war community. With the law enforcement of local counties lying in the hands of a compromised few, the Sheriff, it worsened things for the locals. But how truly wild was the West compared to other regions that made up the Americas?

Notable historian Frederick Jackson Turner[1] declared that the Frontier[2] or Old West was a potpourri of cultures, a melting point of savagery and civilization[3]. Thus, the old West experienced a high degree of struggles to establish cultural dominance, property ownership, and profiteering.

There is no point in trying to deny that the West had its share of violence. Two famous incidents to note are the Lincoln County War of the mid-1870s, which resulted in the death of at least 70 people. The second was the O.K. Corral gunfight of October 26, 1881, at Tombstone, Arizona.

However, the general notion that the Wild West was a violent place to live is not an entirely accurate one. You can challenge this notion when you make reference to other counties and localities.

According to 2005 research by John Hill of the PERC[4] Research Institute, the level of unprecedented violence and gang warfare presented in Hollywood movies are very far from the truth. Ironically, the story of America's West was one of cooperation rather than conflict. Although there were pockets of violence in the West, it was not so different than was seen in other parts of the Americas.

For example, in the mining camps of Sierra Nevada, California, and Oregon, there were established rules to guide each miner's operations. With the discovery of gold in 1848 at the Sutter Mill area, there was an influx of people. PERCs identified that at least 300,000 people made the move to California

---

1.   https://www.britannica.com/biography/Frederick-Jackson-Turner

2.   https://www.loc.gov/rr/european/mofc/whitehead.html

3.   https://www.jstor.org/stable/40467257

4.   https://www.perc.org/2005/07/17/old-west-violence-mostly-myth/

from 1846 to about 1860 in search of wealth and a better life. However, there had been earlier discoveries of gold in North Carolina in 1799 (Charlotte Mint) and in Georgia in 1828.

No doubt, this situation only portends the struggle for limited resources. It only gives credence to the argument of violence in the Old West.

The area attracted people of different nationalities and backgrounds to co-exist in the same locality. Every one of these immigrants was armed with s six-shooter while taking part in the gold rush. However, one positive aspect was that the mere thought that the other person was also armed served as a deterrent to violence.

Making the trip to New Mexico, like John and Collins did, to California, Oregon, and other mining camps was usually peaceful. Though there were minor skirmishes or pockets of violence, it was not significant enough to term the West as "Wild," especially when compared to other regions in the Americas.

Regarding violence and life in the Wild West, experienced wagon train historian John R. Phillip, says it was mainly a life of sharing as against dividing, an era of accommodation instead of discord. The westerners had limited access to the legal system; therefore, the notion of concurrent ownership with Native Americans prevailed. They promoted social peace as against internal disharmony.

In a nutshell, the Wild West truly wasn't as violent as we have always been made to believe. At least, not so different from what was experienced in other parts of the Americas. Ironically, available statistics from the U.S. Department of Justice[5] and other expert opinions tend to show higher cases of violence today in New York, San Francisco, Chicago, and Los Angeles than there was in the Old West.

The towns with notoriety or seasonal violence in the Wild West where guns or street fights occurred include the Tombstone. Even Tombstone had a gun control policy to help stem the tide of violence. Licensed gun owners were not allowed to bring weapons into Tombstone; instead, they had to surrender all weapons at a designated location before entering the town. Other areas prone to some level of violence include Kansas, Dodge City, Ogallala, Abilene, Waco, Texas, Nebraska, and modern-day Oklahoma, which was then the Indian Territory.

We can, however, single out Texas as a region with high gun fighting incidences in the Wild West. This is because there were more shoot-outs there than in other areas in the West.

As for the Native Americans,[6]Ian[7] (2018) of the Vintage News says they were mostly friendly and accommodating, unlike what's portrayed in movies. They were not so much land grabbers or gunslingers. Also, there were lower cases of homicide, mass hangings, or gun-boats in the West compared to other regions or as shown in movies.

On the contrary, Native Americans were more hospitable and ready to trade with the immigrants instead of attacking their caravans.

Life and Survival in the Old West

The West represented many things to many people. It was a symbol of hope and marked the rise of America's industrialization[8], a place to make ends meet. But surviving in the West

---

5.   https://www.ncjrs.gov/pdffiles1/Digitization/196196NCJRS.pdf

6.   https://www.thevintagenews.com/2018/01/11/wild-west-myths/

7.   https://www.thevintagenews.com/2018/01/11/wild-west-myths/

was pretty tough. As such early times, life in the West was still primitive with extreme weather conditions. Weather conditions also changed significantly during the summer or winter seasons.

The West was quickly attracting a lot of attention due to the completion of railroads leading out there. Its business interests revolved around the gold mines and agriculture. Other retail businesses and services were prevalent in the West, though, like restaurants, lodges, and more. However, this business interest also brought with it some level of conflict and the survival of the fittest.

Other forms of workers include wagon drivers, farmers, homestead ranchers, infantry, and other unskilled workers. Immigrants also took a share of the local workforce. They worked at the mines as well as pursued other means of livelihood. For example, the Central Pacific Railroad in California attracted a lot of immigrant Chinese, Irish, Germans, and Japanese in search of labor. The agricultural sector also attracted a lot of participation from the outside into Fresno, San Francisco, and Imperial Valley.

Therefore, you would find people living in small hamlets or settlements. Those working in the mines lived in small shelters until they could return to their families in the towns. In other situations, residential tents or camps in mining locations end up becoming small towns or shanties. These dwelling locations at first were not so organized and lacked town planning. It took some planning to get these little shanties properly delineated into blocks of buildings and streets. From such settle-

---

8.   http://www.loc.gov/teachers/classroommaterials/presentationsandactivities/ presentations/timeline/riseind/west/

ments, the towns continued to expand with the construction of more homes or makeshift abodes.

The railroad construction and operations gave rise to more homes. Over time, some of such residences were sold off to other residents and eventually became a part of the towns. Thus, most old west early residences had a lot in common in terms of structure.

Within the Old West towns, you would come across small businesses like the saloon, bars and inns, retail stores, and more. Most of these small businesses were set up by Irish or German immigrants. The entrance of the saloon usually had a front display window for the sale of tobacco products. You could walk into the main room for a drink, as it houses a bar with a limited number of seats for guests. Slightly larger buildings can house saloons, sample rooms, or shops (retail stores). There would be several rooms for drinking, lodging, and more. You have the wine room, party rooms, an open floor for card games, ladies' lounge, and more. The main floor of such buildings served as bars for drinking. Customers were entertained with movies or dance halls.

America's Homestead Act of 1862[9] gave rise to the establishment and ownership of lands for agricultural purposes. Each recipient or family got as many as 160 acres of free land, on the condition that they would develop it for another five years. With such vast expanses of land, the owners required more hands to cultivate it. Therefore, with the development of settlements, people spent their spare time at the local hangouts, drinking, smoking, gambling, and brawling. Females without the wherewithal took to prostitution to make a living. All such activities in the West made it prone to violence and intermittent fights.

The Great Western Cattle trail made places like Dodge City, Kansas, an appealing location. It was the gateway for large herds of cattle and the cattle trade in the West. The cattle trade resulted in the establishment of shantytowns, inns, saloons, and brothels. The high trade interest also attracted outlaws to increase the level of insecurity and lawlessness in the area.

One reason the West served as home to outlaws was the lack of adequate resources for law enforcement. Besides a lack of funding, situations became even worse as some Sheriffs connived with other gangs to perpetrate crimes and social vices.

Native Americans and the Wild West

Native Americans[10]were the first people to occupy the Americas, including the Old West. They worked as ranchers, cowboys, horse traders, horse breeders or horse wranglers, healers, fur trappers, Army scouts, leatherworkers, and more. Native Americans were more peace-loving and accommodating to the visiting groups into the West. They lived in communities, and were more organized and hygiene-conscious than immigrants. This made it easier to engage in bilateral trades with the new settlers.

The new settlers were mostly from Europe, or if you like, the "Old World," who migrated to the New World (America), including parts of the Old West. White settlers came from the east to occupy the areas of the Mississippi. They were involved in mines, ranching, and farming. Others attracted to the West

---

10.   https://iowaculture.gov/history/education/educator-resources/primary-source-sets/westward-expansion-and-native-americans

then included the African-Americans and Chinese as railroad workers.

As a result of the influx of such a diverse amount of people into the West in the mid-19th century, pockets of conflict were created in different locations. The Native Americans gradually lost the battle against the invading tribes and the U.S. As of the 1880s, the Native Americans had very small territories fully occupied by them. Based on the Indian Removal Act of 1830[11], the Native Americans were relocated either by cooperation or forcefully from their initial settlements.

The Cowboy Experience in the West

Over the centuries, cowboys have stood as a symbol of the Wild West. It all began in the mid-19th century and depicted a hero or glamorous picture, but that was so far from reality.

John Joshua rightly noted that the life of a cowboy in the West was an arduous one, filled with hard work. They experienced economic hardship, poor living conditions, and long hours of hard labor. It might interest you to note that cowboys were not the general name as it is used today. When a person was referred to as a cowboy in the Wild West, it meant he was a rustler, outlaw, bandit, horse thief, or desperado. Hardworking and honest cowboys were then referred to as ranchers, cowhands, herders, cowpokes, cowpunchers, and buckaroos. These are the legitimate Cowboys of the Old West[12].

Movies tend to paint the cowboy picture as one of either ranchers or violent people. Some of the earlier notable cowboys were poor. One account stated that the Spanish Vaqueros were

---

11. https://guides.loc.gov/indian-removal-act

12. http://www.american-historama.org/1881-1913-maturation-era/cowboys-of-the-old-west.htm

about the first known cowboys and introduced cattle rearing to the West. This account is quite understandable when you consider the fact that Spain colonized the area in the 1500s. However, another report identified the Texas cattle help as being the first set of cowboys. Over time, the African-American cowboys[13] also infiltrated parts of the Old West during the late 19th century. Some of them came into the region with white settlers as slaves. As of the 1830s, the population of slaves in Texas [14]increased due to the demand for slaves in the south[15]. These cowboy settlers established and cultivated cotton farms and cattle ranches.

Therefore, Cowboys in the West were generally not outlaws or bank robbers, train robbers, or gangsters. They were also not necessarily involved in terrorizing the city or notorious for reckless killings. True, there were always pockets of violence and vices amongst cowboys, but it was not a daily occurrence. However, there was enough gang and gun fighting to keep the locals concerned and feeling threatened.

It took till about the mid-19th century for the Wild West to gain its reputation as a place for violence. Arguably so, these were the years immediately after the American Civil war. This era gradually gave rise to the period of the cowboys. Therefore, the 1860s till the 1890s were the prime years of the Wild West.

---

13.   https://www.smithsonianmag.com/history/lesser-known-history-african-american-cowboys-180962144/

14.   https://www.tsl.texas.gov/exhibits/annexation/part2/question2.html

15.   https://exhibits.library.unt.edu/httpsexhibitslibraryunteduslaverytexas/brief-overview-slavey-texas

One visible fact to note about cowboys of the 18th and 19th centuries is the lack of cleanliness. It could be quite understandable, considering the way of life of cowboys in the West.

Their life was hard and challenging. Cowboys traveled miles under the scorching sun daily. They had to put up with wearing thick clothing with long sleeves and at high temperatures. Cowboys had limited access to water, so not a lot of baths. Not bathing for days or weeks is more than enough to produce repulsive body odor.

The cowboys also had their share of violence in the Wild West. For example, Nat Love[16], an African-American, talks about his experience in the West as a cowboy and a gunslinger. In 1907, Nat was born in Nashville, Tennessee, but lived in Dodge City, Kansas, spending time at dance halls, gambling houses, and saloons. On some occasions, Nat worked as a rancher, transporting a large number of cattle for grazing. But he had to gunbattle with Native Americans in defense of their land. In his spare time, he participated in shooting sports, roping, dare-devil rides, or went drinking with Billy the Kid in the saloon.

The American Civil War and the Wild Wild West

In the mid-19th century, the West was a popular breeding ground for cattle and cotton in the Americas. With the rise of the population of the Old West, white settlers from Texas, in particular, joined the union to participate in the American Civil War.

At the end of the Civil War, much of the population of the West still possessed arms. Having very little to do after the war, the armies worked on farms and carried out any available

---

16.   http://docsouth.unc.edu/neh/natlove/natlove.html

task to survive. Therefore, white settlers took advantage of the armies to claim lands from the Native Americans.

The white settlers left their farmlands and herds in the hands of the black slaves until they returned from the Civil War. But due to the poor terrain and lack of fencing, a lot of cattle ran wild. Also, the Emancipation Proclamation (immediately after the Civil war), gave slaves their freedom. The white, therefore, had to employ the services of African-American cowboys to help round up their cattle. The African-Americans also worked as cowboys, chasing and leading the cattle to shipping locations in Kansas, Missouri, and Colorado. These shipments do not go without attacks from cattle hustlers or Native Americans, and surviving the harsh environmental conditions was difficult. Black cowboys also had to deal with the issue of racism.

In a nutshell, the Old West has all the trappings of a developing society in its crude state. Conflict was also one of the challenges of civilization and socialization, which was also one of the problems faced in the West. However, to declare the West as a notable place for violence would not be totally accurate.

Chapter Two: Worst Kid to Babysit

Talking about the Outlaws of the Wild West, we are going to start with a focus on one of the most notable outlaws of all time, Billy the Kid. What makes Billy an unusual character and a must-read is that he represents a group of people whose choices and circumstances in life helped to determine their life outcomes to some extent.

Billy the Kid, as he is popularly called, also went by the name Henry McCarthy. Another pseudonym he used was William H. Bonney.

I don't suppose seeing Billy the Kid show up as one of the infamous outlaws will appear surprising to you. No doubt, he is arguably one of the most notorious outlaws of the Wild West. His entire life story began and ended abruptly within approximately two decades. He was feared by some, wanted by some, including the law, and loved by some more.

Several notable books have been published about Billy the Kid. Dozens of movies and documentaries exist about this onerous character and Wild West outlaw. His fame within the West knew no bounds, to the extent that there are many names he was popularly called. In the 1920s, Billy the Kid was known in some quarters as the "Robinhood of the West." Others referred to him as the "Homicidal Maniac," "Frontier Superhero," and the "Murdered Symbol of Freedom." It is this last representation with the freedom I find hard to understand.

Early Life of Billy the Kid
Billy the Kid was more or less an everyday kid who's poor living circumstances and birth directed the path to what he

eventually became. He was a young orphan who, in a bid to make ends meet, had a not-so-pleasant romance with the law. Ironically, for a notable outlaw, Billy the Kid did not have such a negative record to show. There were no cases of bank or train robberies credited to him. However, he had enough going on to constantly put him on the wrong side of the law and at the center of gang warfare.

There are some discrepancies about Billy's date of birth, as records indicate he was born either September 17 or November 23 of 1859 or 1860. However, one thing is certain, and that is that Billy the Kid was born in New York.

Billy the Kid grew up in a poor Irish community on the East Side of New York[1]. But he preferred the name William H. Bonney as opposed to his birth name of Henry McCarty. He went by Bonney, which was his mother's maiden name, Catherine Bonney. The name William came from his stepdad, William Antrim.

Billy never had a real father figure, as his biological father disappeared from home, leaving him in the custody of his mom. William Antrin was a stern stepdad who never really cared about Billy or his brother, Joseph.

Billy the Kid Moves West

The challenges of life made it necessary for the whole family to relocate to the West. In 1865, Billy, Joseph, his mother, and stepfather, Antrin, made the long trip to Indiana[2]. After five years (1870), the family continued their genesis to Wichita in Kansas[3].

---

1.   https://www.britannica.com/place/New-York-City

2.   https://www.history.com/topics/us-states/indiana

3.   https://www.history.com/topics/us-states/kansas

Further evidence pointed to the fact that the family made another relocation to New Mexico[4]. It was in New Mexico territory, however, that Catherine and William Antrin officially got married in 1873.

An unfortunate incident occurred in 1874 that redefined Billy's life forever. And that was the death of his mother in Silver City. Some accounts state that she died of lung cancer while other records have that it was Tuberculosis.

With his mother dead, his stepfather never really paid much attention to the two brothers as he moved on with his life after the burial of Catherine. The kid had to move into a boarding facility to continue his lonely life at the young age of 15. The death of his mother, however, had an adverse effect on him. Billy became timid, afraid of life, and desperate.

A Life of Crime Begins for Billy the Kid

Barely one year after Billy's mother's death, he and his brother started stealing food to survive. Billy started advancing in crime. He teamed up with Sombrero Jack, another local thief and thug to steal from a local Chinese laundry. Billy hid the cash, clothes, and two guns in the boarding facility where he lived.

Unfortunately, while Billy was hiding the bag under his bed, he was discovered. Therefore, the landlord immediately reported him to the police.

Billy received light sentencing as the law enforcement officer only wanted to keep him locked up for about three to four days before releasing him. That seemed too long for Billy, so he made his escape through the chimney of the facility. His details were published in the Silver City Herald over the issue of his

---

4.   https://www.britannica.com/place/New-Mexico

escape from jail. This began his life as a fugitive of the law, and his journey in and out of one prison. In most cases, he had to gain his freedom by escaping out of jail, and not because the law let him go.

After Billy made his escape, he headed out to his stepfather's place to lay low. When he told his stepfather all that happened, he scolded him and sent him packing.

Billy Takes a Job and Ends up with His First Major Crime

Billy never had any form of formal education or vocational skill. However, upon his move to Arizona territory, Billy took up menial jobs as a ranch hand, though his earnings all ended up in gambling instead of improving his standard of living.

While going about his activities at a regular inn located in Bonita Campground, Arizona, Billy was constantly mocked and made fun of by a blacksmith named Francis Cahil. On one occasion, Billy retorted at Francis, calling him a "son of a bitch" for referring to Billy as a "pimp." This got Francis infuriated. He made an attempt at Billy, pushing him to the floor in the inn. It was at this point, Billy removed Francis' gun from the upholster and shot him, fatally injuring him. Billy made a quick escape before anyone could get hold of him, while Francis eventually died from the bullet wounds. Billy again became a fugitive of the law, this time for committing his first major crime; murder.

Billy, John Tunstall, Sheriff William Brady and the Lincoln County War

After Billy escaped from Arizona, he headed out to New Mexico. He eventually moved to Lincoln County in 1877 in search of a means of livelihood. Billy was again fortunate to find work as a farmhand for John Tunstall, who was barely six years older than Billy. Tunstall was an English businessman and rancher. It didn't take long for Billy to become close to Tunstall and eventually became his personal bodyguard.

Life in Lincoln County was like every other locality in the West, fuelled by competition and survival of the fittest. Every business owner strove to control the market and increase profitability. John Tunstall had a partner and lawyer known as Alex McSween. Their fiercest rivals were Irish businessmen, Lawrence Murphy, and James Dolan. However, both parties have had business dealings in the past, and McSween was indebted to Dolan to the tune of $8,000. The value of that sum by today's standards is approximately $200,000.

Most notable businessmen in the West had their law enforcement teams, and so was the case in this county. Dolan wanted the debt repaid by any means. Through the aid of Sheriff William Brady, he made an allegation against John Tunstall in an effort to bring down his business. Sheriff Brady shut down Tunstall's business, confiscating his livestock, which was worth over $40,000, which would be somewhere in the neighborhood of $980,000 today.

When the Sheriff came along with legal documents to inform Tunstall (and possibly close down the business), he was met with fierce opposition. William Brady later sent some men to arrest and shut down the business, and a fight ensued between Tunstall's men and Dolan's thugs. This resulted in the death of Tunstall, as he was shot at the back of the head with his personal rifle. And so began the journey to Lincoln County War.

Billy on a Revenge Mission: The Regulators

Billy the Kid was with John Tunstall at the time Dolan's group shot him dead. He, however, could not do much to save Tunstall then, but he vowed to get justice for his former boss and friend.

Billy the Kid went to the Lincoln Country justice system to ask for the prosecution of Dolan and William Brady over the murder of John Tunstall. In a sudden twist, the justice department commissioned Billy to effect the arrest of the Sheriff and Dolan.

When Billy approached Brady with his arrest warrant, he, Dick Brewer, and another cowboy ended up being arrested by the Sheriff. The Deputy U.S Marshall locked the trio up for some days, but eventually let them loose. When Brady saw that the legal system did not have the necessary force to bite, he was determined to see Brady pay for the murder of Tunstall.

It didn't take long before Billy and some friends established "The Regulators." The Regulators were former employees of John Tunstall who took it upon themselves to fulfill the role of independent law enforcers in Lincoln County.

Such acts only helped to overheat the polity as other business interests and their law enforcers would be affected. Dolan and Sheriff William Brady did not take the activities of The Regulators lightly. Thus the actions of Billy the Kid and his Regulators resulted initially in the death of two of Brady's men. Further attacks between each team finally culminated in the death of Sheriff William Brady.

Brady's death sparked a series of violence, known as the Battle of Lincoln, which began on July 14, 1878. Both parties went all out to eliminate members of the other group. Unfortunately, local law agencies did not do much to save the situation. The gun battle went on for at least five days before the U.S. Army Squadron came in from Fort Station to take charge.

The security operatives and the rival gang wanted Billy and the former regulators to surrender, but no, they preferred to shoot their way out of the situation. McSween's home was set ablaze while the shooting went on.

In the ensuing battle, McSween was murdered, but Billy and some of his team members made it out alive and headed out of town. The authorities had to step into the situation to avoid further breakdown of law and order in the county. Therefore, a peace accord became necessary to prevent further bloodshed. However, it could be assumed that the Dolan/Murphy teamwork of the battle since Tunstall and McSween died as a result of the feud. At last, the Regulators were disbanded by the authorities based on a conspiracy involving other rival groups. Members of the Regulators were later referred to as outlaws and banned from Lincoln County, including Billy the Kid. No judgment, arrest, or form of punishment was meted on the Dolan team and members of The Home.

By the end of the Lincoln County War, at least 70 people had lost their lives in the violence.

Billy the Kid and Governor Lew Wallace

New Mexico Governor Lew Wallace later granted pardon to all those who participated in the Lincoln County War. However, Billy the Kid was the only outlaw *not* granted a pardon by the state. All outlaws without a conviction received a total pardon.

Billy later made friends with Dolan and the Home. But to ensure total loyalty, the group signed a pact of secrecy and that anyone who broke the accord would be put to death. They decided to drink to celebrate the new agreement, but Billy stayed away from drinking. When they stepped out of the building, Jesse Evans, one of the outlaws, got into an argument and accosted a fellow and shot him to death following a disagreement. Billy witnessed this incident and quietly ran out of town instead of sticking to the pact with his new team.

Once out of town, Billy maintained correspondence with Governor Lew Wallace. He offered to testify against Jesse Evans on the grounds that the Governor would grant him pardon. I suppose Billy was tired of a life of crime and being a fugitive. He longed to live as a free man again. Wallace accepted Billy's offer and they arranged a meeting and staged his arrest.

The law enforcement officer tracked and arrested Billy to avoid any suspicion of conspiracy and to protect him from rival gang attacks. Billy testified against Jesse Evans and his new friends. Thus he broke the pact between them. By agreeing to testify, Billy took a significant risk because these gangs were powerful, and could sometimes infiltrate the legal and security systems to get at anyone.

Billy expected to gain his freedom after his testimony, but he was a long way from freedom. The judge was brought in from outside the county and would not hear of any agreement between Wallace and Billy. Governor Wallace rode off immediately after the trial without honoring Billy's get out of jail free card. Billy wrote several correspondences to Governor Wallace, reminding him of the pact and the need to keep his end of the bargain to no avail.

As was his nature, Billy again broke out of jail on June 17, 1879, to reclaim his freedom. He eventually ran off to New Mexico, like he always did.

Henry McCarthy, a.k.a Billy the Kid: The Journey to the End

Billy the Kid lived a life of violence. He would shoot first and think later. He, however, had to lay low to avoid the long arm of the law. But the law finally caught up with him on December 23, 1880. Sheriff Patrick Floyd Garrett [5]and his team of law enforcement officers apprehended Billy in Mesilla, New Mexico, and brought him back for trial. Billy was found guilty of murder and sentenced to death by hanging on April 31, 1881.

After almost two years of violence and killings, Billy was only charged for the murder of Sheriff Brady, irrespective of the spate of shootings and killings he was involved in. Ironically, of all the parties involved in the Lincoln County War, Billy was the only outlaw ever apprehended and charged. Of course, some of the others without an earlier conviction got a pardon from Governor Wallace.

One account states that the seating judge reiterated that Billy was going to hang until he was "dead, dead, dead." And Billy retorted with, "You can go to hell, hell, hell." However, there is no evidence to substantiate this claim in official records. You can only find that line in the movie: Young Guns II of 1990. It's possible the lines were only contrived in the head of the scriptwriter.

So, could this be the end of the road for Billy? No, die-hard Billy the Kid would not go down so easily. In his usual nature, Billy broke out of jail again, but not until after killing the two deputies assigned to restrain him from escaping. He asked to use the restroom. On the way back to his cell, Billy charged at the guard, grabbed his six-shooter, and fired several deadly shots. The second guard heard the gunshots from across the street and came running to the rescue, only to fall prey to Billy's bullet. Billy was in a better position as the guard was down on the street while Billy stood upstairs at the balcony. The shooting attracted the attention of bystanders, but they all took to their heels. Billy immediately ran to the horse stable and rode off, never to return to Lincoln County (or so he thought).

Sheriff Pat Garrett was out on an official assignment when Billy carried out his escape plan, but he was not going to give up on the chase so quickly. Garrett spread his dragnet across Lincoln County to New Mexico and beyond. He swore Billy the Kid would not evade him this time around. Meanwhile, Governor Wallace had placed a $500 bounty on Billy, dead or alive.

Garrett spent several months trying to track Billy down. With a tip-off from some of Garrett's contacts, he set out to apprehend Billy by laying an ambush for him at Fort Sumner, New Mexico. His two deputies, Thomas McKinney and John Poe, went with Garrett on this important, albeit dangerous mission.

Garret traced Billy to Maxwell Ranch in Fort Sumner. He initially tried getting information from the locals there, but got nothing useful. This is because the residents liked Billy, and he seemed to be a fun-loving person. Pete Maxwell is a former acquaintance of Garret and a friend of Billy. Garrett knew that if there was anyone who could give him useful information, then it was Peter.

Pete confirmed that Billy was in town and came to his place regularly. While asking Pete about the current whereabouts of

Billy, Garrett heard a knock on the door, and the voice of Billy, asking who was in the home with Pete. It is unlike Billy to hesitate if he felt something was out of place. He typically shoots first and asks questions later. I guess he assumed that it could have just been his friend, Pete, in the dark. However, Pat Garret, in his book[6], *The Authentic Life of Billy the Kid,* gave a vivid account of what transpired that night.

On July 14, 1881, Sheriff Patrick Floyd Garret brought down Billy the Kid with barely two shots from his pistol. At the young age of 21 years, one of the most famous outlaws of the Wild West, met his waterloo. Billy the Kid, Henry McCarthy, a.k.a, William H. Bonney, met an abrupt end.

One perceived motivation for Sheriff Pat Garrett's desire to see Billy put to death was his resolve to clean the polity of crime. Or could it be the Sheriff had a pact with one of the rival gangs seeking to bring Billy the Kid down? Whatever the case, there was also the issue of financial reward - the bounty for Billy the Kid. Ultimately, the $500 reward was not given to Garrett by the government. It is quite understandable, considering he was supposed to be representing the law. However, Pat Garrett did receive a $7,000 reward from Messila, Santa Fe, Las Vegas, White Oaks, and other cities in New Mexico for bringing an end to the menace of Henry McCarthy. The $500 rewards were finally released in 1882 through a legislative act.

There have been questions about the authenticity of Sheriff Garrett's claims of killing Billy the Kid in 1881. Several arguments claim that Billy survived the attack and made an escape that night. Some people have also said they saw Billy the Kid

---

after that, or that they actually were Billy, without any proof to substantiate the claims.

For an outlaw, Billy the Kid had no history of robbing trains or banks like most outlaws. His major crime was killing Sheriff William Brady and the other two deputies. Not like killing these law enforcement agents wouldn't stand as a heinous crime. But when viewed from the prevailing circumstance, (when the authorities issued Billy to arrest the Sheriff and his cohorts), it becomes a different issue altogether. Governor Wallace was on the verge of issuing a pardon to Billy, but not much is clear as to why he finally refrained from doing so. Could it be assumed that the governor didn't want to go down in history as the person who granted a notorious outlaw the freedom to roam the streets again? When you consider the fact that he did the same for others involved in the Lincoln County War, it leaves room for unanswered questions.

The Governor of New Mexico, Bill Richardson, rejected a request for the pardoning of Henry McCarthy in 2010 on the grounds of ambiguity about what transpired. This pardon would have been in line with Governor Lew Wallace's initial promise to William Bonney.

Billy may have been killed that infamous night in July, but the events surrounding his death did not die so fast. Besides claims of Billy resurfacing, later on there were also unsubstantiated accounts of how he escaped death that night. Historian Robert Stahl sought (but to no avail), the issuance of a death certificate[7] by a New Mexico court just to end the issue of Billy being alive.

---

7.   https://www.history.com/news/historian-seeks-death-certificate-to-end-billy-the-kid-rumors

Controversies surrounding Billy's life and death still persist. One of such conspiracies is Ollie Brushy Bill - Roberts claims to be Billy the Kid in 1950 in Hico, Texas. He, therefore, sought a pardon from New Mexico Governor, Thomas Mabry.

However, friends and other residents at Fort Sumner came out to see that Billy the Kid had been killed that night. Also, the $500 reward to Sheriff Pat Garrett was only issued after a Coroner's report was approved by the New Mexico legislative arm. A six-man coroner's jury was set up to review the event on July 14. They were said to have examined the corpse of Billy the Kid, the crime scene, and then interview Garrett and Maxwell. After that, their report confirmed that Billy the Kid was indeed the person shot by Sheriff Garrett.

Billy the Kid, a.k.a William H. Bonney remains a notable feature of the Wild West movies with at least 50 movies shot to his credit. At Hico, Texas, there is a Billy the Kid Museum that tells the story of his escapades. In conclusion, I dare say one lifetime is not enough to live the life of Billy the Kid, considering his anecdotes.

"The hardest decisions in life are not between good and bad or right and wrong, but between two goods or two rights"
- **Joe Andrew**

Chapter Three: Bold and Bad and Brave

The popular axiom, when life gives you lemons, make lemonade, is nowhere near true about the life of our next outlaw of the Wild West. In a nutshell, he was a direct opposite of Billy the Kid in terms of his background, family upbringing, social status, and his family's spiritual standing. Jesse James is the son of a pastor from a good home with a higher social status. Billy the Kid could only wish for a similar experience, but their actual early lives were miles apart. Jesse James' parents were loving and could afford most of the basic necessities of life. It is a wonder how someone born into such a home ended up becoming an outlaw in the real sense of it.

Billy the Kid had no history of train or bank robberies, except horse rustling and gang rivalry. But Jesse James went all out into crime. He became a bandit, train robber, and bank robber, involved in multiple shootings, among other crimes to his credit. However, in a related twist, Jesse James is seen in some quarters as a Robin Hood sort of character. We shall explore how true that is in the course of this chapter. But one thing is clear, and that is that Jesse James was an outlaw and a known leading member of the James Younger Gang of Outlaws. The life and times of Jesse James are immortalized in the "Ballad of Jesse James[1]," where it was said, "Jesse James was bold, bad and brave."

Early Life of Jesse Woodson James

---

1.   https://www.nationalgeographic.com/history/magazine/2019/01-02/infamous-missouri-outlaw-jesse-james/

Jesse Woodson James was born near Kearney (formerly Centerville), Clay County, Missouri, on September 5, 1847. Jesse's dad, Robert James, was a reverend gentleman of the Baptist church who married Zerelda Cole James. In 1842 the family decided to relocate from Kentucky to Missouri to continue ministerial work and build a business. Kentucky was actually the native home of his parents.

Zerelda gave birth to three lovely kids, namely Frank, Jesse, and Susan. Jesse was the second child of the three kids. Alexander Frank was the first, and Susan was the third child (and only female) born to Reverend Robert James.

Jesse's father ran a hemp farm with about six slaves who helped with the operations of the farm. His father also played a major role in the establishment of William Jewell College, located in Liberty, Missouri, once they arrived in town. The family spent quality time in Missouri while the family's farm business continued to grow.

Jesse and his siblings were given a good education in relation to what was obtainable in the 19th century. Taking into consideration their social status and appearance, there was no evidence to suggest that the blue-eyed boys, Jesse and Frank James, would end up as outlaws. He had all the trappings of a boy who would grow up to become a fine gentleman. Ironically, Jesse and Frank James turned out to be one of the most notorious pairs of outlaws in the West.

In 1850, Reverend Robert James continued his ministerial work and headed out to the gold mining camps of California to minister. Unfortunately, that was the last time the family ever set eyes on their husband and father alive. Reverend Robert fell ill and died, due to an undisclosed ailment, not long after his arrival at the camp.

Tales shared amongst family members indicated that little Jesse held unto his dad's feet and pleaded with him not to embark on the journey. Before his death, he had maintained correspondence with the wife and kids, always asking about their welfare and sending personal advice. He would say, "take a portion of it (his love) to yourself and kiss Jess for me," "tell Franklin to be a good boy and learn fast." Being a minister, Roberts usually added, "I must close by saying live prayerfully and ask God to help you train your children in the path of duty."

Though far away from home and in pursuit of his ministerial call, Reverend Robert James obviously had a heart for his family, but his desire to see more souls share in his Christian faith was paramount to him. He said with the influx of people into the California mines during the gold rush; there was an opportunity for a harvest of souls.

Jesse James' parents met in the summer of 184 when Zerelda was barely 16, and Robert was 23 years. By December that same year, the pair had become husband and wife. Jesse's father was a Georgetown College student when he met Zerelda, who schooled in a Catholic school in Lexington. An account by a former classmate says Robert was a gawky and timid kid in school, and that resulted in his being ridiculed often. However, over time he became popular and well-liked in the college due to his easy-going nature.

A visit to Zerelda's parents in Missouri was all that Robert needed to make the decision to stay there and raise a family with his young bride in West Missouri. Clay County was serene, fertile and would make a good ministerial location. Robert acquired 225 acres of land in Clay County, Missouri, for his residence and farm after completing his bachelor's degree on June 23, 1843, in Kentucky.

Reverend Robert became a minister at the New Hope Baptist Church. When he joined the church, the congregation was about 20 members, but at the end of seven years, the congregation had hit approximately 300 members. It appears the missionary calling Jesse James' dad made it impossible to stay in a place for too long, even after having kids. Thus, his journey to California became his last missionary trip.

Jesse Woodson James: Family Life, Values

Strong-willed and outspoken, Zerelda Cole James was a devoted and caring mother. She gave her all to see her kids grow up strong. However, her fortune began to change over time with the demise of her husband, Reverend Robert, and Zerelda was faced with deep financial burdens.

Zerelda had to remarry a wealthy farmer, Simms, on September 30, 1852, after the death of her husband, Reverend Robert James. Jesse's new stepdad never really liked or cared for the boys. Simms, Jesse, and Frank James were always at loggerheads over several issues until he eventually sent them packing. Zerelda didn't take lightly to his actions and decided to leave the marriage. However, her second marriage actually ended abruptly as Simms fell off a horse on one occasion, and that led to his final demise.

Zerelda remained in James' family farm to cater to her three kids and ensure the farm remained productive. She, however, made a third attempt to find love again by marrying Reuben Samuel in 1855. Samuel would be her third and last husband. But to ensure the marriage was for all the right reasons, Zerelda made Reuben sign a prenuptial agreement. Reuben Samuel is also a native of Kentucky and a practicing medical doctor. Zerelda went on to have four more kids with Samuel, bringing the total number of children she bore to seven.

Jesse James grew up in a warm and caring family until he was almost 15 when the events surrounding the civil war redefined life for him. However, growing up during the slave era gave Jesse firsthand experience of the impact of slavery on people's lives.

Most of the earlier values learned by Jesse were obviously modeled from home. Being a minister's son must have also taught him some useful lessons in his contact with the church. But how those experiences played out in later life never really reflected in his anecdotes.

In Missouri, Jesse James had an education but also had ample time to play around and be the little boy he was. Clay County had a large expanse of lands, fields, and woods, and they formed playgrounds for the young lad and his siblings. However, as much as he had time to enjoy nature and the basic necessities of life, western Missouri had a fair share of slave workers, totaling about 2,742 in 1850. Jesse spent the better part of his growing up days assisting with the tobacco and hemp farm. On most occasions, he assisted the family slaves to get the job done and in lifting the family income.

American Civil War and the Seed of Violence

Jesse James was in his early teens (13 years) when the American Civil War[2] broke out from April 1861 until April 1865. It

---

2.   https://www.britannica.com/event/American-Civil-War

was the unprecedented level of violence and shedding of blood that influenced Jesse James to aspire to a life of violence, and then later, crime.

The war began as a result of the pro-slavery stance of southern America versus the anti-slavery position of Northern America. The problem of slavery had been a running battle for decades now between the South and the North. The southern economy depended largely on the slave labor force[3] to keep their plantations running. Some of the most popular trades then were incotton[4], hemp, and tobacco. White southern farmers required a large number of personnel to cultivate their farms. Thus, while the South had an abundance of slaves.

Northern American businesses invested more in the transportation systems - railroads, steamboats, canals; and in communications - telegraph, newspapers, magazines, and books. They also invested in the financial industry, including the insurance and banking sectors. Ironically, over 80% of the manufacturing businesses existed in the free labor states of the North. But southern whites were twice as wealthy as northerners in terms of per capita income. As a matter of fact, three-fifths of the wealthiest Americans were from the South. This orientation further helped to widen the gap between the pro-slave South and anti-slavery North.

Most residents of Missouri, including the James family, were pro-confederates with pockets of union supporters within the mix. Jesse James' family arguably had to support the confederates, considering the fact that they are also slave owners with farmlands as well as having roots in Kentucky.

---

3.   https://www.britannica.com/topic/labor-in-economics

4.   https://www.britannica.com/topic/cotton-fibre-and-plant

The conflict over the Civil War was brewing in Kansas territory. The conflict had to do with whether the state would join the Union troops or the Confederate side. However, these controversies seemed far enough from Missouri, but the final outbreak of the civil war did not spare the James family or the state. However, the whole issue of the American Civil War was a litmus test as to whether America was going to evolve as a confederate state with each state having powers to secede from the union or if they would maintain a sovereign government.

The heat of the era was always top of mind for Missouri residents. It was a very controversial issue as residents openly supported either the Confederates or the Union. As one report stated, people were all mixed up, supporting different sides of the war. Others served as a spy for either side. Frank James was reported as saying, "you were for the South, and your neighbor was for Lincoln." Frank James was reported by a neighbor to have gone trigger happy on one occasion. He went, screaming, shooting his pistol, and declaring support for Jeff Davis (the Confederate leader) in the wake of the war.

Jefferson Finis Davis[5] was a United States Senator and a House of Representatives member for Mississippi under the Democratic Party and prior to the American Civil War. He, however, became the President of the Confederate States, which sought to secede from America as the country had become deeply polarized across the pro-slavery and anti-slavery lines.

---

5.   https://www.biography.com/political-figure/jefferson-davis

In 1860, Republican Party candidate Abraham Lincoln[6] won the U.S. election to emerge as the 16th President of the United States of America. Abraham Lincoln recorded 40% of the electoral votes from 18 states, 180 Electoral Votes, and 1,865,908 popular votes to emerge the winner of the presidential election.

The elections fielded candidates from four political parties. John C. Breckinridge from Kentucky contested under the Southern Democratic Party with 18% electoral victory from 11 states, 72 Electoral votes, and 848,019 popular votes. Stephen A. Douglas from Illinois contested under the Northern Democratic Party with 29.5% of the total votes. He secured 12 Electoral votes, won only in one state, and a total of 1,380,202 popular votes. John Bell from Tennessee contested under the Constitutional Union to secure 39 Electoral Votes, three states, and 590,901 popular votes to garner 12.6% of the total vote cast.

In actuality, the 1860 US presidential election was the major catalyst of the American Civil War. It was clearly evident to the Confederate states that the new government was not out to serve the interest of a select few, but rather an idealized American nation. Lincoln was born in Hodgenville, Kentucky, but hails from Springfield, Illinois, and understood some of the travails of the region.

Thus, Confederate President Jeff Davis, from Christian County, Kentucky, initiated the process for the secession of seven states from the United States of America. The seven

---

6.   https://www.whitehouse.gov/about-the-white-house/presidents/abraham-lincoln/

Southern states included Alabama, Florida, Georgia, Louisiana, Mississippi, South Carolina, and Texas.

In his inaugural speech, President Abraham Lincoln gave a stern speech stating that "in your hands, my dissatisfied fellow-countrymen, and not in mine, is the momentous issue of civil war. The government will not help you. You have no oath registered in Heaven to destroy the government, while I shall have the most solemn one to preserve, protect, and defend it."

All these actions only helped to further overheat the polity as the tension became palpable. That was the condition Jesse James lived in as a teenager, with fears of possible attacks on their county from Union troops or skirmishes between the Confederates and the Unionists.

Finally, on April 12, 1861, Confederate forces launched an attack on Fort Sumter[7]. The Fort was one of America's coastal defense points, close to Charleston, South Carolina. Abraham Lincoln already had plans to send in resources to beef up supplies at the Fort for eventual battle. But the Confederates General P.G.T Beauregard laid a siege on the garrison. For nearly 34 hours, there was a constant exchange of artillery fire with an estimated 3,000 rounds fired by the Confederates. Bullet-ridden with fire until Major Anderson and his troop of about 85 soldiers surrendered to the Confederates on April 12, 1861. This singular incident marked the beginning of the American Civil War.

Over the following weeks, more states switched loyalty from the Union to join forces with the confederates, and they include Arkansas, North Carolina, Tennessee, and Virginia.

---

7.   https://www.history.com/topics/american-civil-war/fort-sumter

As things kept snowballing out of control, President Lincoln requested for and recruited at least 75,000 personnel to join the war for three months. The Confederates, on their part, recruited 100,000 militiamen (later increased to 400,000) for six months to take up arms against Union troops. These spates of polarization and gunbattles marked a phase of endless violence and tension, which over the next four years was to claim the lives of over 625,000 Americans; civilians, military, and foreigners.

The American Civil War was the most devastating and largest conflict in America's history between the 1815 Napoleonic Wars to 1914 World War I. Although the Union troops won the war, the battle not only claimed the lives of the Americans but twisted the minds of Jesse and Frank James. Violence for Jesse and Frank James became second nature, something that happens naturally without recourse as to the action, implication, or justification.

Jesse Woodson James: Pushed to the Wall

Jesse James was barely 14 years when the American Civil war commenced; therefore, he was not yet of age or permitted to participate in the war. However, his brother Frank James, who had already turned 18, excitedly enlisted as a pro-Southern Missouri State Guard. Frank took part in two notable battles in Missouri. They were the Lexington and Wilson Creek battles, eventually won by the Confederates. He only had five months of service before he was brought down by measles and admitted into the military hospital.

Unfortunately, Federal forces, also known as Jayhawkers, were already onto Frank, and he was arrested and granted parole after signing an oath never to take up arms against the Union.

The American Civil War got bloodier, claiming lives across the South and North. Missouri became an epicenter of violence and bloodshed. Inhabitants took sides with the Confederates and Unionists. Combatants from both sides took to the streets, woods, and fields. They strategized, confronted, and neutralized their enemies - fellow Americans. They raided towns, killing both civilians perceived to aid the opposition, taking no prisoners but going for summary execution. Once they laid hands on the opposition, they were captured, tortured, and taken back to base.

The situation attained such an astronomical height that even the young, able-bodied men felt the hot rush to fight for what they believed.

Frank James could not resist the urge to go back into a full combatant. Therefore, in May 1863, he joined the Southern guerilla forces under the command of William Clarke Quantrill. This was in direct violation of his parole agreement with the Federal forces. The Southern guerilla also went by the name "Bushwhackers." They were a team of independent cavalry troops with shared ideologies and sentiments of the Confederates. Their modus operandi all depends on the whim and caprice of Quantrill. The Bushwhackers got funding from family and friends as well as intermittent raids around Missouri.

Willam Clarke Quantrill was a teacher prior to the Civil War. He signed up with the Confederate Army in 1861 before jettisoning for his independent militia forces in 1861. Quantrill had over 600 troops loyal to him, including Jesse James' brother, Frank James. One of the most notorious incidents credited to the Bushwhackers was the Lawrence Massacre of August 21, 1863.

William Quantrill, alongside Frank James and over 400 troops launched an assault against Lawrence County, Kansas, killing over 150 males, most of them civilians. Quantrill was a bloodthirsty fellow on a mission. Frank James recalled about Quantrill, "we knew he was not a very fine character... but we wanted to destroy the folks that wanted to destroy us, and we would follow any man who would show us how to do it." That's how much negative influence Frank James, and later Jesse James, were exposed to.

Jesse James Gets His First Share of Violence

Frank James became a notable name amongst the guerillas, and it didn't take long to attract the attention of the Union. In May 1863, the Unionists headed out to the James family farm, hoping to apprehend him at home. Unfortunately, Jesse James and other members of the family had to deal with the situation as Frank was nowhere in sight. Convinced that the bushwhackers must be around the area, the Unionists gave Jesse James the beating of his life for refusing to divulge any information. What more could run through the mind of an innocent young lad in his mid-teens, seeing such a monstrous show of hatred and the willingness to take human life over a difference in ideologies?

As if that was not devastating enough, Reuben Samuel, Jesse's stepfather, became the next target. He was badly beaten and then hung on a tree until he agreed to lead the team to where the bushwhackers had their camp.

This was a case of operation take no prisoners, as immediately the Jayhawkers (Unionists) confirmed the location of the guerrillas, they opened fire at random on the camp. Two men dropped then on the spot, but Frank narrowly escaped unhurt, with bullets riveting through the air like fireworks. It must have been a horrific experience, having death staring at you from all angles, with no concrete plan of action, but just the need to get out and stay alive! Frank stated several years later, that day's experience had redefined life and existence for Jesse James. He said, "Jesse was out for blood[8]."

In the meantime, Jesse returned to his life at the farm, tending to his parent's tobacco plantation. At the young age of fifteen, Jesse James was already burdened with the thought of revenge, but he had to wait patiently for the perfect time to come while harvesting crops alongside their seven slaves. It didn't take long for the opportunity to present itself. By the following winter, the bushwhacker guerillas were in dire need of recruits. This time, the farming season was not going to stop Jesse James from enlisting as a guerilla fighter. So began Jesse Jame's life of violence!

There are several accounts as to how dastardly Jesse James became, killing at will and always armed when stepping out. From the year 1864, Jesse James had only two things in mind, revenge and bloodshed. One account in 1864 showed how he allegedly took out revenge by killing Brantley Bond. Brantley was one of the union militia who tortured his stepfather. When the bushwhackers apprehended Bond, he immediately surrendered and began pleading for his life. Jesse was said to remind the militia of his earlier escapade with Jesse James' family and then shot him.

---

8.   https://www.nationalgeographic.com/history/magazine/2019/01-02/infamous-missouri-outlaw-jesse-james/

Next, it was Frank James' turn to take on a revenge mission. With the aid of other bushwhackers, Frank apprehended Alvin Dagley while he was at work in a field near his home. They dragged him onto the street, and Frank immediately shot him to death. Frank says many years later about the incident that, "we did burn the houses of Yanks... we shot spies, and so does everybody. If we hadn't, we wouldn't have lasted a week."

The James brothers were on a path of violence. It would appear it became quite easy for them.

On September 27, 1864, Jesse and Frank James joined ranks with another team of bushwhackers led by Anderson. Commander Anderson, also known as "Bloody Bill," gained notoriety for the callous manner in which he removed the scalps of his dead victims or union soldiers. On the said date, a team of bushwhackers laid siege on a train approaching Centralia, Missouri, killing 24 Federals who were onboard the train, leaving no prisoners. The officers coincidentally arrived in town while the troop was on a rampage. Anderson and his team wasted no time in getting rid of them. On another incident that same day, the bushwhackers got intel that a couple of federal troops had arrived in town in an attempt to trail guerillas. Jesse James led the pack of guerrillas to launch an attack on the federals. He galloped at top speed towards the union commander, knocking him off his saddle and simultaneously fired at the commander's head. The entire troop of bushwhacker guerillas had followed Jesse closely and immediately opened fire, killing almost the entire troop of 115 union soldiers.

Jesse James gained popularity, authority, and admiration amongst the simple folk of the town who share the sentiments of the confederates. Every single battle increased his fame and the desire to conquer more territories. However, commander Anderson never made it alive from Centralia. He died in July in the course of a skirmish.

Jesse James Takes Another Bullet to the Chest

Jesse James and the bushwhackers returned to Missouri during the spring of 1864. They killed, maimed, and looted towns just to keep the battles going. At this time, the war wasn't looking so good for the confederates. General Robert E. Lee had recently surrendered to the Union troops at the Appomattox Court House. This sentiment was also evident in the desperation amongst the bushwhacker guerillas, who were making every effort to keep the battles on the winning side.

On May 15, Jesse's encounter with Federal patrols close to Lexington, Missouri, almost brought an end to one of America's most infamous outlaws. Jesse came in a direct confrontation before Federal patrolmen, and in the course of the ensuing violence, a bullet ripped through Jesse's chest, piercing his right lung. The bullet hit around the same spot as that of his experience with stealing a saddle one year ago. His injury took longer to heal this time; therefore, Jesse had to lay low for some weeks again, thankful to God for escaping with his life.

The last experience with the Federal patrols turned out to be Jesse James' last combat before he surrendered to the Unionists. There were speculations by his family that Jesse was on his way to surrender to the Federals when his crew was attacked. At that point, there were really very few options left for them. The Confederates were down, the guerrillas were fast losing out on all fronts, and Jesse James had sustained a life-threatening injury and could not remain active in the meantime. He could either die fighting or surrender to the Federals. Jesse chose the latter.

Both the James brothers surrendered to the Federals. Frank again swore an oath of allegiance on July 26 in Kentucky, while his younger brother Jesse was recuperating in Lexington Hotel. It, however, took Jesse about five to seven months to fully recover from his injury before returning to Clay County, Missouri. He relocated from the hotel to stay with his uncle for the remaining part of his recuperation. It was in the course of his recuperation that he met his cousin, Zerelda Zee Mimms, who was responsible for nursing him to health.

It would be okay to say something happened between Jesse and his mom's namesake at that time, as some few years down the line, Jesse James married his cousin, Zerelda, from whom he had two kids. That period of recovery was, however, the longest time Jesse James stayed away from crime or warfare since he took up arms against the unionists and since his teenage years.

Jesse and Frank James: A Life of Crime

Jesse James is arguably the most notorious outlaw and criminal in American history. He became a terror to financial institutions and money trains. At an earlier stage in his life, he was a horse rustler, but as events evolved, he moved higher, taking on one bank or train robbery to another.

The years between 1869 to 1881 were the peak for Jesse James' robbery escapades. He was said to have been involved in at least 20 robberies[9] executed on stagecoaches, banks, and trains. From Mississippi down to West Virginia and finally Minnesota, Jesse and his gang of thieves carted away at least $200,000. Approximately 20 persons also fell to Jesse James'

---

9.   https://www.biography.com/crime-figure/jesse-james

bullet, until he was eventually killed by another outlaw, who turned out to be his partner in crime. Thus Jesse James and other outlaws earned the reputation of "Robber State" for the state of Missouri.

One of the earliest horse rustling experiences that comes to mind was in 1863. Jesse had tried stealing the saddle of a German Unionist farmer. Jesse noticed that the saddle was left unattended and decided to sneak into the yard to make a quick getaway! The German Unionist farmer sighted Jesse from the doorway and took a quick shot at him. The bullet missed Jesse's heart but hit the right chest. He was fortunate to make a quick escape to spend the next few weeks recovering from his wounds.

Upon Jesse's return after the war to Clay County, Missouri, it felt strange not going back to a life of peace and quiet. To make matters worse, the Federal supporters still held onto the memories of the Civil War in relation to the pro-confederates. Life after the war was unbearable. There was a new amendment written in 1865 against slavery. President Abraham Lincoln's Emancipation Act brought an end to slavery.

However, to serve as a check on the pro-confederates, there were restrictive laws to avoid a recurrence of the issues that led to the civil war. The Ironclad Oath of 1864[10] restricted anyone who fought for, supported, or had any lining with the southern ideology. The Ironclad law made life more difficult for a society on the road to recovery from years of devastation, killing, and wanton destruction of life and property. It was impossible to secure a teaching appointment, hold public offices, or even

---

10.   https://www.visitthecapitol.gov/exhibitions/timeline/lawmakers-loyalty-and-ironclad-oath-1864

vote during elections without meeting the requirements of the Ironclad law.

Thus former guerrillas and their relatives became disenfranchised in Missouri for some time. Things remained cloudy until the Senate made some adjustments to the Ironclad laws. But by that time, some of the pro-confederates had gone about making their own rules. While some confederates adjusted to the new way of life, farming looked too slow and boring to Jesse and Franks James. They wanted something more spontaneous, exciting, fire-pumping, adventurous with a touch of violence. Jesse and Frank James took the law into their own hands. And that's how the journey to a life of crime began - train and bank robbery became the order of the day for the duo and the other members of the Jesse and Younger Brothers gang.

Jesse's escapades got to such unthinkable heights that he was alleged in 1874 to have robbed a stagecoach during his honeymoon in Austin, Texas.

Strike When the Iron is Hot! The Jameses on the Prowl!

February 13, 1866, a whopping $60,000 of government bonds and the gold currency was stolen from the Clay County Savings Association, and 10 to 12 men were responsible for the act. The funds accounted for mostly the savings of Union militia and had now been carted away by a handful of the ex-confederate militia. One onlooker was shot dead during the course of the robbery. Other than that, it was an almost clean deal.

So began the notoriety and spate of robbery involving the Jameses and Younger brothers. The local press reported the incident, stating that the robbers were former bushwhacker desperados. However, only Frank James took part in the first robbery alongside Cole Younger.

The justification provided by James for choosing the part of robbery instead of returning to their farms or other decent occupation like other confederate militias did was a perceived threat to their lives. Jesse told a reporter that his life was always under threat after his return to the Clay County farm; therefore, he had no other choice. "I was forced to go heavily armed at all times." Frank argued that it was impossible to return to a normal life like every other person, "tilling our farms and being decent as a tallow dog chasin' an asbestos cat through hell." Speculations also went that Jesse argued that bank and train robbery was easy money, and that's something they were good at securing.

Based on some accounts, Jesse went by the nickname "Dingus" due to a mishap with his pistol. He reportedly earned the nickname after shooting off the tip of his finger while cleaning a pistol. Because he didn't like to curse, he said: "That's the doddingus pistol I ever saw!"

However, "Dingus" was just one amongst many aliases used by Jesse due to his lifestyle. Other aliases include John D. Howard, Thomas Howard, Charles Lawson (from Nottingham, England), William Campbell (Texas cattleman).

Jesse used his aliases convincingly to the point that his son, Jesse James Jr., was made to believe his name was Tim Howard until after his dad's demise, when he learned his true surname. Jesse Jr. also reported that his dad, on some occasions, limped or walked with a cane as a disguise.

Jesse James' First Robbery

There were several robberies linked to Jesse, but none of them can be substantiated. One example is the Russellville, Kentucky robbery of 1868. Jesse, Frank, and Cole Younger were said to have robbed a bank. However, there is no evidence of such an incident.

Some other stated robberies involving Jesse might be true, but due to the lack of evidence linking him to such crimes, they ended without a trial; just as slippery or elusive as Jesse James. That is because the aftermath of the war produced such hardship that a life of crime appeared simpler for some warfighters. There were huge losses on both sides of the Civil War, but the individuals felt hit the most. Other guerillas and independent militia groups took advantage of the situation to become outlaws, robbing for a living.

However, on December 7, 1869, the Daviess County Savings Association robbery had Jesse's name written all over it. It was an operation tagged by many as an assassination rather than a robbery. Jesse and another fellow walked into the Daviess County Savings Association located in Gallatin, Missouri, and shot the cashier on duty without any provocation. They only picked a small metal box of cash before fleeing the scene. The duo fled the scene on one of the horses instead of the two separate horses they came on initially. Jesse's horse was in no mood for a quick getaway as it forced the rider off by throwing tantrums.

While making the run, the robbers were said to have boasted to onlookers that they did put an end to Major Samuel P. Cox, the militia commander who killed Bloody Bill Anderson. Thus, this could be more of a reprisal attack for the murder of the bushwhacker leader during the Civil War. Well, whether that was the original intention of the duo, it was a case of mistaken identity, as they ended up killing the wrong man. The robbers killed John W. Sheets, and not Cox, as presumed. The mare racehorse left at the crime scene by the bandits provided evidence as to who committed the crime. The racehorse was known as Kate and belonged to Jesse James.

A jury was set up to investigate the robbery. In May 1870, Frank and Jesse James were tried for the murder of John W. Sheets. Jesse immediately wrote a letter to the Governor of Missouri. In his defense, Jesse stated that he had no hand in said robbery or assassination, and that he can provide his alibi to prove his innocence. Jesse, however, stated that he would only make himself available for interrogation when he is convinced he will get a fair trial instead of a witch hunt. Jesse retorted, "I will never surrender myself to be mobbed by a set of bloodthirsty poltroons." One way or another, the Kansas City Times, edited by Edward John, gained access to a copy of Jesse James' letter and got it published. This marked the beginning of a series of publications about the James brothers.

At some point, bank robberies were looking a bit more problematic; therefore, the James and Younger brothers focused more on train and stagecoach robbery. Train robbery seemed a lot easier to execute with little or no resistance. One account stated that the brothers could sometimes raid a train in public glare. Jesse was noted to enjoy the publicity and attention to the extent he started distributing leaflets about their crimes to onlookers. Similar to what is referred to in today's corporate world as a press release. If Jesse's publicity stunt didn't get enough public attention, Edward Newton's media coverage definitely did achieve that purpose.

James Brother's Train Robbery

In January 1874, Jesse and Frank, in collaboration with their gang, accosted a train at Gads Hill, Missouri, carting away huge sums of money. Unlike other robbery incidences, this one refused to go unresolved. The Pinkerton National Detective Agency (PNDA) was contracted to investigate and hunt down the criminals. It is a private agency with expertise in preventing and tracking train robbery. The bank was established in 1850 in Chicago by Allan Pinkerton, a Scottish immigrant. He was the pioneering detective of the Windy City Police who helped southern slaves escape via the Underground Railroad. Allan Pinkerton used his expertise as a detective in uncovering an assassination plot against President-elect, Abraham Lincoln. Also, his intelligence-gathering prowess was instrumental to the federal government during the American Civil War.

The agency took on the chase of the criminal with all seriousness. But the criminals were not going to sit back and allow themselves to be apprehended. In March 1874, one of the Pinkerton detectives was found murdered without clear evidence as to those responsible. Another detective was killed while on the trail of the James associates, Cole and Robert Younger.

Arresting the James' brothers, Younger brothers, and others were not going to be an easy task, but Allan Pinkerton became all the more resolved to see these die-hard criminals brought to justice.

One year later, the hunt for the James and Younger brothers was still going. On the night of January 25, 1875, selected Pinkerton agents were sent out on their pursuit. They acted based on a tip-off from an unnamed source and stormed the James family farm in search of Frank and James. Their mother has always been an ardent supporter of the duo and was home with the other family members when the detectives decided to raid the home. To avoid an unexpected attack or the escape of Jesse and Frank, the agents launched an incendiary device on the property that resulted in an explosion that rocked the foundation of the property. The main targets, Jesse and Frank, by a stroke of luck, were not home, but the explosive led to the death of their 8-year-old half brother, Archie Samuel. Their mother, Zerelda, also was a victim of the assault as the explosive took off part of her arm. Zerelda had to undergo surgery to amputate the arm from the elbow.

The attack on Jesse and Frank further turned the brothers into a hero in the eyes of the public to the extent that some members of the state legislature considered the possibility of granting the duo amnesty. Jesse and Frank were not known to forgive a perceived offensive. They rode on the wings of public sentiment to spot the Pinkerton agent informants who aided their preparations for the attack. The informant was a nearby neighbor and an ex-Union militiaman. Once they could spot the information, the brothers shot him dead in April. As things got messier with pursuing the James' brothers, Allan Pinkerton decided that it was time to lay the issue to rest.

Not this Time Around! A Failed Robbery Attempt

As much as it appears that the James' brothers were daredevils and unstoppable criminals, they finally met their match on September 7, 1876. Jesse and Frank James, along with Cole, Robert, and Jim Younger, as well as three other gang members, stormed the First National Bank of Northfield, Minnesota. They got wind of the fact that a former Republican governor of Mississippi during the Reconstruction era had relocated to Northfield. Adelbert Ames came with Benjamin Butler, his father-in-law. They both were staunch Unionist and Republican political figures.

The gang attacked the First National Bank of Northfield based on a tip-off, which indicated that the men had deposited huge sums of cash to the tune of $75,000 in the bank.

Three of the gang members walked into the bank to survey the internal situations and be sure everything was safe. The trio approached the cashier, demanding he open the safe, but the cashier refused. People around the bank suspected that a bank robbery was in place, and the news went viral. Armed men of the town came to the rescue leading to a gunbattle between the men and the robbers stationed around the bank.

With the sound of gunshots outside, the three robbers inside took a shot at the cashier, killing him on the spot before running out of the banking hall. As the battle got all the more fierce, a passerby was gunned down by the robbers while two of the robbers were killed by the townspeople. Jesse, Frank, and the remainder of the gang took to their heels unhurt.

Barely two weeks after the failed robbery of the First National Bank of Northfield, the Younger brothers came under attack at Madelia, Minnesota. The James brothers had separated from the Younger brothers; therefore, they were not named in the ugly incident.

During the ensuing gunbattle, one member of the gang was killed while the Younger brothers were captured and sentenced to life imprisonment. In 1889, Robert Younger died still serving his jail term while Cole Younger was released on parole in 1901.

The James brothers, as always, escaped any implications over the failed bank robbery. Therefore, they saw it necessary to go into hiding for some years. The duo took up pseudonyms and relocated to Tennessee to avoid the law.

At this point, Frank James decided he has had enough of the bank, train, or any form of robbery. But it appears Jesse was doomed to a life of crime because he only lay low for a few years and then in 1879, put together another group of criminals. Thus, Jesse was back on the highway and Railtrack again, doing what he knows how to do best; robbery.

After their initial success, this new set of gang members didn't seem to have the magic that gave the winning string of each robbery. It didn't take long to disband some members of the team for different reasons. Several people joined and left the Jesse James gang within a short time. Other challenges experienced with the new gang were internal wranglings and the lack of trust, the latter of which would become Jesse's undoing. Of all the members of the gang, Jesse only had much confidence in Robert and Charley Ford because of their links with some old guerilla friends.

Is Jesse James a Robin Hood alias?

The notion of Jesse James as a Robin Hood of some sort has no substance anywhere in history. Robin Hood[11] is English folklore about an outlaw who specialized in robbing the rich to redistribute the proceeds to the poor. From all Jesse and Frank James's stories, there are no actions or nothing in their ideologies pointing to that.

Jesse James and his Wild West crew were branded as Robin Hood type figures due to the effort of Editor John Newman Edwards. Edward had a sentimental liking for the Jesse James

---

11.   https://www.nationalgeographic.com/history/magazine/2019/01-02/origins-of-england-folk-lore-robin-hood/

character, and through his news articles, painted a picture of a Robin Hood, robbing the rich to feed the poor. His support for the Jameses is quite understandable considering the fact that Edward was an ex-Confederate officer and a Democrat to the core.

In some of his publications, Edward alleged that Jesse James deserved the name Lancelot and King Arthur in playing the interesting role of Spinoff, a popular Outlaw in King Arthur's Court. "They are outlaws, but they are not criminals," reported Edward.

Edward also went on to endorse Jesse James as a Southern Hero during the fall of the Civil War when the outcome and reality of the war were biting hard on everyone. Jesse, on his own part, sent in letters to the newspaper organizations to always explain issues and state his innocence or provide justifications.

Another possible reason for the speculation that Jesse James was a Robin Hood could be when Jesse offered to send money to a parent whose daughter he accidentally shot during a robbery in the Kansas City Exposition with the public outcry over the robbery that resulted in the shooting of the little girl. Jesse or his gang member wrote a letter for publication using a pseudonym. He apologized to the family requesting they send their address through the pages of the local city Weekly Times so he could send a refund for the medical bills.

How Jesse Woodson James was Eventually Murdered

Finally, another American Outlaw from the Wild West meets his waterloo at the age of 34. At the productive and ripe age of 22, Jesse James became a notorious outlaw. He spent the next 12 to 14 years robbing banks, trains, and other innocent victims. For him, there was always a justification for his action, and with a promise of a fair trial, he would make himself available, so he said.

Jesse, Frank, and the Younger brothers were the most sought after, the most despised, but still the most celebrated outlaws.

James Woodson James, I suppose, was never meant to die in a bank or train robbery or quit the life of crime. Therefore, it took a fellow gang member to put an end to the legendary outlaw.

On Monday, April 3, 1882, Robert Newton Ford and brother Charley Ford paid a visit to Jesse James at his home, located at 1313 Lafayette Street, St. Joseph, Missouri. The trio conversed for some time over breakfast while the rest of the family were in other parts of the home. The discussions got a bit uncomfortable as Thomas Howard (actually Jesse James) talked about the surrender of a fellow gang member, Dick Liddil, to the authorities. Dick Liddil was a horse thief who recently joined the gang through the Fords. Jesse exclaimed that Liddil was a traitor who deserved to be hanged. Little did Jesse know, sitting before him were worse traitors.

The trio made their way to the stable at the back of the house to see the horses. Once back in the living room, Howard (Jesse) exclaimed that it was hot indoors and therefore took off his coat and tossed it on the chair nearby. He also removed his pistols, considering he was in his own home. Howard noticed some dirt on the photo by the wall, reached out for a duster, and stood on a chair to clean it. The two brothers immediately seized the opportunity to round Howard up on both sides. Charley winked at Bob with Howard's back turn toward them. The duo pulled their trigger, pointing it at the back of

Howard's head. As soon as he heard the sound of a cocking gun, Howard began to turn his head when Bob took the shot. Charley never took a shot but watched as Howard, real name Jesse James, dropped to the floor with a bullet to the head.

As Jesse James turned his back to his friend in an attempt to straighten a photo on the wall, Robert Ford brought out his trigger, aimed the pistol at his boss's head and pulled the trigger. Howard's wife was attending to other personal business within the home when she heard the loud bang of the gun and came running to the living room. Immediately she stepped into the room she saw the brothers still standing, holding a six-shooter. Robert and Charley explained that the gun accidentally went off. An account of the incident said Zerelda calmly bent over her husband and said, "Yes, I guess it went off on purpose," meaning she did not believe their story. But her action is quite understandable because seeing that these men killed her husband, she couldn't raise an alarm and risk having been killed by them, too.

Robert and Charley left the crime scene and headed off to the nearest telegraph office just down the street to send a message to sheriff Henry Timberlake of Clay County, to let him know of the development. They also made contact with the Kansas City Police Commissioner, Henry H. Craig, as well as the Governor of Missouri, Thoman Crittenden. The last person the duo reached out to was the Office of the City Marshal, Officer Enos Craig.

Robert Ford could not resist the promise of huge reward and amnesty for his own crimes as a ransom for the murder of Jesse James. Robert and Charley were relatively young members of the gang, joining a little over a year before the time of Jesse's death. Though they had become acquainted with Jesse in 1879, it took longer before the opportunity to join forces came. The duo succeeded in gaining the trust of Jesse due to their links with a former Confederate militia and guerilla, John T., who turned out to be their father. Robert had worked out the terms of the assassination with his elder brother, Charley, so that they could take the reward and put an end to their criminal activities.

To fulfill their plans, Robert Ford had earlier that year made an arrangement with the Governor Thomas Crittenden of Missouri, to capture or assassinate Jesse James in exchange for amnesty and financial reward. That is why they immediately sent word across to the governor about the incident. However, security operatives arrested Rob and Charley, and they were arraigned for murder. On April 17, 1882, the duo was tried for first-degree murder and sentenced to death by hanging. Governor Crittenden immediately stepped in to grant them a pardon. Unfortunately, the Ford brothers never got the financial reward they expected for delivering Jesse James dead instead of captured.

Governor Thomas Crittenden, during his election campaign, made a promise to apprehend and rid the state of the notorious criminals and outlaws, Jesse and Frank James. To achieve this, he brought stakeholders and company executives from the railroad and express company to work out a resolution. The executives understood that the activities of the James brothers were a threat to their business; therefore, a total reward sum of $50,000 was realized to put an end to the gang. Jesse and Frank James each had a reward of $5,000 on their heads. The assailants must capture and submit them to earn the reward. There was also another $5,000 for conviction. Thus the information about the bounty for the heads of the duo circulated across the state of Missouri. What seemed unclear was whether Jesse James was needed "Dead or Alive," but I guess the boys felt only death could deliver Jesse to the authority!

The death of Jesse was a blow to a section of the public and undoubtedly Editor Edward Newman. But the media didn't let Jesse James rest even in death as for several months unending; the newspapers had fresh reports for publication raking in sales.

Robert and Charley Ford went ahead to reenact the killing of Jesse in roadshows with the admiration and criticism of members of the public. Robert Ford was seen as a coward for killing Jesse in the manner he did. However, it didn't take more than two years (1884) for Charley Ford to commit suicide for undisclosed reasons. Jesse's murderer, Bob Ford, was shot dead by an unknown assailant in 1894 while in a saloon located at Creede, Colorado.

However, there were speculations that Jesse James possibly faked his death to bring an end to that ugly episode of his life. Some people toiled with the possibility that a different person was buried and not Jesse James. Like in the case of Billy the Kid, several individuals surfaced claiming to be Jesse James. An example of such an impostor is Frank J. Dalton in the early 1950s.

Over the years, Jesse's tomb became a tourist attraction, and his mother, Zerelda, charged a quarter every time a tourist sought to take a pebble from his graveside. More people profited from the life, death, and times of Jesse James. Zerelda Howard (Jesse's widow) had to sustain the family after his murder, for 6-year-old Tim Howard or Jesse Edwards and 2-year-old Mary Susan. Zee sold off some personal effects belonging to Jesse and the family just to keep things going. Their favorite dog even had to be sold.

Their home became a tourist attraction as Zee charged 10 cents per admission into the facility. Souvenir hunters had a field day chipping off parts of the fence or building just to have some artifact of Jesse James. Jesse's property owner, Henrietta Saltzman, dragged the Missouri state government to court over complacency in his murder. Mrs. Saltzman moved back into the property and was alleged to have made a fortune selling artifacts of the building to more tourists, charging as much as $1,500 for souvenirs. Jesse's rent was only $14 per month, but in death, his landlady generated almost ten years' rent over the life and times of the legendary outlaw and from a single tourist visitor. A local reporter pointed out that Mrs. Saltzman claimed that there were over 50 bullets from the Jesse James murder found in the home, well there is no evidence or autopsy to support this claim.

To clear the air on the true identity and final resting place of Jesse James, in 1995, scientists carried out a full coroner inquest and autopsy of the corpse. There were photographs already taken off the corpse earlier that helped to check or validate the claims. His corpse had initially been moved from its original resting place in the James family farm to Mt. Olivet Cemetery at Kearney, Missouri. Robert Ford's tomb carried the unpleasant inscription: "The Man Who Shot Jesse James." What was written on Jesse James' tomb, showed how much admiration he enjoyed: "In Loving Memory of my Beloved Son, Murdered by a Traitor and Coward Whose Name is not Worthy to Appear Here."

Finally, the DNA test laid to rest every assumption, as it was the remains of Jesse Woodson James that were buried, meaning he was actually killed and buried, as stated in earlier accounts.

The End of One of America's Legendary and Infamous Outlaws

No matter what, Jesse James seemed to have the respect of some segments of society. Editorials paid much attention to the enigma and mystery surrounding the James brothers. Over time, authors and movie theatres saw their story as an exciting one to talk about. Their robberies provided intriguing pieces for audience consumption with some exaggerating occurrences and events just to spice things up a bit.

As if the media attention was not bad enough, at some point in Jesse James' bank robbery incidents, there were reports of him printing leaflets for distribution around the scene of the crime. The flyers stated that a group of young men came into town, robbed a bank, and successfully got away with huge sums of cash.

Some segments of the public, on the other hand, didn't seem to mind about the robbery group, as long as it was not them under attack. Jesse James and the Young brothers' public sentiments and goodwill and wish them a prosperous life in good health. Thus, Jesse James has earned his place in a countless number of films and fictional and historical literature of America, particularly about the American outlaws. His reputation is ironclad to the point some refer to his murderer, Robert Ford, as a coward for shooting him from behind.

The life and times of Jesse James were reenacted in countless movies, telling the tale of one of America's infamous outlaws of the West. Jesse's son took part in two of such movies in 1921 titled; "Jesse James as the Outlaw" and "Jesse James under the Black Flag" where he played the role of his father and of himself, the son.

In a nutshell, the impact of the harshness of slavery and the high level of violence and bloodshed had reconditioned the mind of Jesse, gradually pushing him to accept killing as a way of life. These and other events caused him to become a vengeful person. He killed at will anyone who fell within the bracket of the Union. He, however, took to a life of crime and had ready answers or justification for his actions. Hence, Jesse was prompt to seek pardon or provide an explanation to the public for some of his actions as if there could be a moral justification for such actions.

Justifying Jesse James' life, Editor John Newman Edwards argued that Jesse and Frank could be classified as "bad citizens because they live out of their time."

To, however, say societal actions and occurrences pushed Jesse James into a life of violence, and horrendous killings would not be entirely inaccurate, but to justify the events that led to his eventually becoming an outlaw would be given moral justification for willful criminal acts.

"The choice to make good choices is the best choice you can choose. Fail to make that choice and on most choices, you will lose." - **Ryan Lilly**

Chapter Four: The Mexican Robin Hood

The legend of Robin Hood has been a part of human history for decades now. The story has been told in a different way by historians, storytellers, and moviemakers until it became a household tale. But have you ever heard of Joaquin Murrieta Carrillo? Well, he might not sound so familiar to you unless you are a student of history, media practitioner, or more. However, I'm sure you are probably familiar with Deigo de la Vega of the Legend of Zorro.

This chapter looks at Joaquin Murrieta Carrillo, who was an infamous Mexican American outlaw and a Robin Hood of his day. He, however, might not strike you as the regular or notable outlaw in the public domain due to poor documentation about his anecdotes. Joaquin, besides being termed an outlaw, is also known as The Robin Hood of the West. Others refer to him as the Robin Hood of El Dorado.

His life makes for an exciting read, with a career in the robbery, horse theft, and murder on one side or an activist advocate for justice. However, your assessment will depend on the angle you choose to see Joaquin, as he is generally perceived from two distinct perspectives. Some see him as a hero, the hero of Mexican Americans in California, others see him as an outlaw and a bandit.

Early Life of Joaquin Murrieta

Joaquin Murrieta Carrillo was born around 1829 in the northwestern part of Mexico, known as the Sorona, Mexico[1].

---

1.   https://www.britannica.com/place/Sonora

He was baptized barely one year after his birth, still in Sorona. One historical account by Frank Forest Latta[2] puts the place of his birth as the Hermosillo in Pueblo de Murrieta. He resides in the Rancho Tapizuelas near the Cuchujaqui River, on the north of Casanate and southeast of Sorona and the Sinaloa border, which is currently the Alamos Municipality, Mexico.

There are no clear indications of where he stayed while growing up, as not much is known about Murrieta. The irony of it all is that Murrieta's life story has become so twisted that you might end up with inaccurate information about the legendary outlaw due to the myriad of conflicting stories projected through movies, novels, and myths.

Joaquin Murrieta did have a bit of an education close to his community at a place known as El Salado. He, however, was not from a financially stable family; therefore, he had to start working to earn a living quite early in his teenage years. Not much is mentioned about his family background, but he lived amongst his relatives, and the fact that he had stepbrothers indicates that one of his parents remarried at some point while he was growing up. His baptism at the age of less than one year also indicates that he is likely from a Christian background.

Murrieta had an early marriage while in his teens to Roza Feliz and had to start working early in his teenage years. He was a fine and hardworking young man who tried to fend for his family. Several factors in Murrieta's life pointed to the fact that there were close ties between him and other members of his immediate and extended family, and we shall explore two of them now. Some of the other factors will play out when he gets to California, as well as portrays what eventually pushed Joaquin

2.   https://en.wikipedia.org/wiki/Frank_Forest_Latta

Murrieta into becoming an outlaw (or an activist, if you see it that way!).

The California Trip and the Gold Rush

In 1848, Murrieta's older stepbrother, Joaquin Carrillo, sent him a letter. Carrillo, at this time, had relocated to California and was already working in goldmines. In his letter, he described to Murrieta the situation he was currently in, as well as about the discovery of gold (the California Gold Rush[3]). Carrillo explained to Murrieta the prospects of making it big in California by prospecting for gold. For a young, hard-working teenager, it didn't require much convincing to tell that Murrieta would accept his offer when Murrieta Joaquin Carrillo finally encouraged him to come to California.

Thus, by 1849 Joaquin Murrieta, his lovely wife, Roza Feliz, as well as dozens of other relatives and friends, were ready for the long trip to California to get their fair share of the California Gold Rush. Other accounts stated that they made the trip either in 1849 or 1850. But one fact remains clear, and that is that Murrieta made the trip to California at the fall or wake of the 1840s/1850s, respectively. But seeing that Murrieta had to deal with the issue of Foreign Miners Tax in 1850 makes 1849 look more like the appropriate year the party made the trip. Also, there were variations in the different accounts on the number of persons that made the trip to California.

They had to make the journey like many others from Sorona, via the Altar and Colorado desert[4] to get to California in the Americas. All those in Murrieta's traveling party included Murrieta's younger brother, Jesus Murrieta, and a Carrillo

---

3.   https://www.britannica.com/place/California-state/History#ref79270

4.   https://en.wikipedia.org/wiki/Colorado_Desert

stepbrother, Jesus Carrilo Murrieta. He also had three in-laws (his wife's brothers) in the crew; Claudio, Jesus, and Reyes. There were also two cousins named; Martin Murrieta and Joaquin Juan, and two cousins of Valenzuela named; Jesus Valenzuela and Joaquin Theodore. The Duarte cousins, Manuel and Antonio, also made the large family train as well as other friends and men from Pueblo de Murrieta and Sorona. Will they get there in one piece, or get burnt along the way?

Fortunately, the party arrived in California without a hitch. They immediately set out to understand their environment and get to work prospecting for gold. But it had to take them some time to settle down. They also had to go through some difficult times trying to adjust to this new place, plus Murrieta never realized that they would have to deal with the issue of racism.

It's time to get rich quick (or so they thought)! Joaquin Murrieta and his wife, Roza Feliz, settled down pretty fast. Murrieta was a devoted husband and a hardworking gold miner. Murrieta, his wife, and some of the brothers immediately built a small home on the hills of Hangtown while working towards a claim. On a daily basis, the team heads out to the goldfields to prospect for gold. Barely one year of coming over to California, Murrieta had started experiencing significant success as a gold prospector. The future of the family was looking a lot better in California.

A Twist of Fate

However, in 1848, the California Gold coast territory was handed over to the United States by the Mexicans at the end of the Mexican-American War. Thus, Mexicans became foreigners in what was initially their own land. Barely one year after the handover, gold was discovered in commercial quantity in the territory in 1849. This discovery resulted in an influx of miners from across the Americas, Europe, and Asia, including the Chinese. The competition became both stiff and fierce as prospecting miners throng the area daily to get their share of the gold.

Resenting the level of competition from every angle, the American miners sought a better way to organize things as well as ensure there was proper regulation of operations across the goldmine. Some sections of the American miners thought it necessary to intimidate and send these foreigners packing. American miners, therefore, came together to enforce these regulations. However, they sought the assistance of the legislators to create laws regulating gold mining operations and possibly licensing in 1850 in Sacramento.

Therefore, in that same year (1850), the Greaser Act[5], as well as the Foreign Miners Act of 1850, came into play. Unfortunately, the Mexicans were worst hit by this legislation. Non-American miners had to pay a tax of $10 per month (which translates to about $330 in today's dollars). They had to obtain licenses and temporal permits to operate, plus meet other conditions for gold mining operations. However, the Foreign Miners Tax was replaced in 1852 with the Foreign Miners License Tax Act at $3 per month. The act also introduced the Miners Tax for foreigners as well. Things got uglier as the American miners kept insisting that foreigners should not be allowed to hold a mining claim. The Mexicans kept working out ways to resolve the issue to ensure they could work without limitations.

Catastrophe Strikes

5.   https://www.britannica.com/topic/Greaser-Act

Joaquin Murrieta and his wife worked hard at the mines and kept experiencing success, but the hostility against them simply refused to abate. One account alleged[6] that a group of American prospectors accosted the Murrietas while at home, requesting he hand over his mining claim, but Murrieta declined. The group became infuriated and began beating Murrieta before tying him up. They also got a hold of his wife Rosita and raped her before him, making him watch the despicable act. Rosita later died of complications and the injuries she sustained from the rape incident.

With the murder of his wife, Joaquin Murrieta lost the will to prospect gold anymore. A report stated that Murrieta quit his claims and switched to card dealings and again became a victim of hostility.

Murrieta Joaquin went on a horse ride on his half-brother's horse to see a friend. On his return, he came across a mob of locals who harassed him, claiming he must have stolen the horse. He, however, insisted the horse was not stolen but refused to disclose the source of the horse until he was whipped severely. The account stated that the mob headed straight for the half-brother's house, forced him out and lynched him immediately without any investigation.

At the same time, the Murrieta brothers kept facing threats over their involvement in the gold prospecting business. They kept trying to surmount the obstacles until it became clear that there was no way forward for them in gold mining anymore until they all lost their claims. Finding work became almost impossible and even risky. One account states that Joaquin Mur-

---

6.   https://en.wikipedia.org/wiki/The_Life_and_Adventures_of_Joaqu%C3%ADn_Murieta

rieta looked at the whole position of things and felt he couldn't stomach the injustice, highhandedness, and mistreatment of Mexicans in California anymore.

All Out for Revenge

Joaquin Murrieta felt pushed to the wall and frustrated, and so sought to seek revenge on all those responsible for killing his wife and brother. Over the next few weeks, every single person responsible for the deaths were going to pay for their heinous crime. One after the other, Murrieta assailed each member of the mob that killed his brothers. They all suddenly began turning up dead with mutilated bodies. Now, he has had his own pound of flesh!

A Life of Crime Begins

Using the excuse of the inability to work and the loss of their claims, Joaquin Murrieta assembled some of his friends, brothers, and contacts. They were going back to the hills and goldmines to prospect for gold again. However, Murrieta wasn't going to stoop for intimidation and the use of legal claims to stop them from mining gold. This time, he will allow the Americans to do the dirty job while he and his gang will "smile to the bank!" Amongst Murrieta's team of raiders included, Manua Garcia, "Three-Fingered Jack," a Mexican army veteran who fought during the Mexican-American War. Three-Fingered Jack was so named due to losing two fingers during a firefight in the course of the war. The group started out by attacking miners coming back from the goldfields, obtaining their gold, and in the face of any hostility, killed their victims. Over time, the group began to attain frightful positions on the hills and area.

In Frank Forest Latta's account, he explained that Joaquin Murrieta and his gang were a group of well-organized raiders. Murrieta led one group of raiders while other relatives and residents from Sorona teamed up to raid Calaveras County in Central California and the goldfield area. These men had helped Murrieta in killing the six men who killed his brother, Jesus Carrillo, after they were accused of stealing the half-brother's horse.

The groups further began an illegal horse-trading business from America to Mexico. They sourced their horses by stealing from other American residents and gold prospectors. Latta writes that the gangs could steal mustangs from farther north regions like Contra Costa County, Central Valley, from the gold camps in the Sierras and transport them through La Verde del Monte, the Diablo Range to head south to Sorona to sell the horses.

When not involved in horse rustling, the raiders regularly robbed gold miners or settlers on stagecoaches. They also kill any uncooperative victim. However, their victims over time were not limited to Anglo-Americans, but also the Chinese goldmines, carting away all their mined gold.

Murrieta's raiders became infamous in the entire territory, instilling fear in the hearts of miners. Their operations covered the entire California goldmine area, San Joaquin, and up to the Sacramento valleys. As the situation got out of hand, the ranchers began complaining to the authorities about the activities of the gang. The raiders would sometimes suddenly emerge from hideouts within the hills and assault their unsuspecting victims. There was no American safe from the Murrieta raiders who purportedly started out on a vengeance mission. Joaquin allegedly serves justice in his own way.

Individual reports also painted Joaquin Murrieta as a Robin Hood of the West. He was said to target gold miners, particularly goldmines that were hostile and exploitative, he robbed them of their gold and then gave it to poor Mexican natives to assist them. These natives also helped to shield him from authority and protect him from any harm. Thus, Murrieta was able to sustain his operations for several years without coming in direct confrontation with the law. Their raids were said to be so successful to the degree that they killed three lawmen[7] without being made to face the wrath of the law.

Joaquin Murrieta was the leader of the Five Joaquins, a group of raiders specialized in cattle rustling, murders, and robberies across the Sierra Nevadas from 1850 to 1853. Members of this elite gang included Joaquin Carrillo, Joaquin Botellier, Joaquin Valenzuela, Joaquin Ocomorenia, and Manual Garcia (Three-Fingered Jack) who is Murretia's, right-hand man. The group was reported to have carted away gold worth over $100,000, killing over 20 men and stealing over 100 horses.

How Murrieta Joaquin Finally Met His End

Joaquin may be the Robin Hood of the West or El Dorado, but to some, he and his gang were a menace. There was a widespread outcry against the group from local miners and even the foreigners under attack. In 1853, the California legislature believed they had seen enough of Murrieta's threat in California and were going to do something about him. There the Five Joaquin bill was passed in May 1853, seeking to bring an end to this ugly episode.

---

7.   https://www.legendsofamerica.com/lawmen-list-a/

The government of California thus contracted 20 California Rangers[8] under the leadership of Captain Harry Love to hunt down the Five Joaquin. Governor John Bigler, therefore, signed into law the "California State Rangers" act for the job. Members of the California Rangers were Mexican-American veterans of war. Captain Harry Love was a skilled soldier, ex-Texas Ranger, and War veteran.

The Five Joaquin have all at one time, or another headed different teams of marauders notorious for horse rustling and trading as well as robbing gold miners.

Captain Harry Love was contracted for a period of three months at a rate of $150 per month plus a $1,000 governor's reward for the capture of the Joaquin Five. Thus began the confrontation between the Mexican gangs and the Rangers. For several weeks the Rangers unsuccessfully tried to apprehend Murrieta and his gang. The first confrontation between State Rangers and a group of Mexican outlaws, however, took place in July. One account, however, stated that the Rangers, on occasion, caught Murrieta's brother-in-law and tortured him till he led the Rangers straight to the hiding place of the outlaws in Cantua Creek.

Thus on July 25, 1853, the Rangers made an early morning attack on the bandits when they least expected it. The incident occurred around Arroyo de Cantua, near Diablo Range and close to Coalinga, California. The gun duel was a tough and lopsided one; Twenty Rangers and war veterans with expertise in tracking and battling Mexican fighters during the American-

---

8.   https://www.history.com/this-day-in-history/california-rangers-kill-joaquin-murrieta

MexicanWar versus a group of mostly young unskilled fighters. The odds were against the Joaquin Murrieta group.

That episode ended with the death of three Mexican raiders. Another account stated that about eight members of the gang were killed that day. However, two notable members of the gang allegedly killed that day were Joaquin Murrieta and Manuel Garcia (a.k.a, Three-Fingered Jack). Another two members of the gang were captured in that same fight.

To show the significance of the event, the state erected a plaque in the location of the fight, marked as California Historical Landmark 344[9]. The plaque stood at state routes intersection 33 and 198.

The State Rangers needed a souvenir to serve as evidence of their conquest. Therefore, the Rangers chopped off Manuel Garcia's hand as well as the head of Murrieta Joaquin to present as evidence. They had to place the hand and head in a jar of alcohol to preserve them. Thus, the evidence was displayed in Mariposa County, San Francisco, and Stockton. To celebrate the unprecedented victory over the outlaws, Captain Harry Love went on a tour around California and beyond to display their reward, the severed head and the arm of the notorious outlaws. Spectators paid $1 just to see Joaquin and Manuel's head and hand, respectively. Joaquin Murrieta is the shortest-lived outlaw discussed in this book of infamous outlaws, due to the twist in his life and story.

Captain Love never met Murrieta in person; therefore, he does not know what he looks like. However, to confirm that it was Joaquin Murrieta and Manuel Garcia that were killed by the State Rangers, a Catholic priest and at least seventeen peo-

---

9.   https://en.wikipedia.org/wiki/California_Historical_Landmark

ple signed attestation that the head was that of Joaquin Murrieta. Not long afterward, Love and the other State Rangers smiled to the bank with their $1,000 reward and other benefits; it was an exciting moment for the team.

In a related twist in August 1853, San Francisco Alta California Daily received an anonymous tip-off from a fellow in Los Angeles. The man claimed that Captain Love and the Rangers only made a fast one on the state. He stated that the person murdered was a Mexican mustang catcher and not Joaquin Murrieta. The secret informant also alleged that those who testified that the murdered fellow was Joaquin only did so after they were promised financial gains.

The Los Angeles claims were just one amongst many more as letters started rolling in from several sources about Love killing the wrong person. Toward the fall of 1853, California newspapers published some of the letters with claims about the incident. Part of their argument was that in Captain Love's display of Joaquin Murrieta's head, he never visited the mining camps to show off his victory. However, other reports indicated that their claims were untrue.

The California State legislature was not in any way swayed by the publications in California newspapers. Therefore on May 28, 1854, the state legislature approved the sum of $5,000 as a reward for putting an end to Joaquin Murrieta and his gang. There were also claims by O.P Stidger in 1879, alleging that Murrieta's sister commented that the head on display by Captain Love was not her brother's. Murrieta's sister explained that there was a characteristic scar on her brother's face that was not present on this head.

Different people also claimed they had seen Murrieta on several occasions, even 25 years afterward. This had always been the trend with the most notable faces and outlaws, though. Even in death, many still refuse to acknowledge the fact that Murrieta was gone. More unsubstantiated reports about seeing Murrieta in different parts of California began making the rounds. Since these claims had no legal backing or proof (like that of Captain Love), there is no basis for accepting them as true.

Joaquin Murrieta's head was later deposited in a bar at the Golden Nugget Saloon, Stockton, San Francisco and was destroyed in the 1906 San Francisco earthquake and fire. Not much was heard about the other Jaoquin outlaws that escaped that day's gunbattle with Captain Love. However, Murrieta's nephew, Procopio, arose in the late 1860s and early 1870s to continue in the stead of his uncle, Joaquin Murrieta. He quickly gained fame as one of California's notorious robbers and outlaws of the 1860s. There were speculations that Procopio heard so much about his uncle and wanted to follow in his footsteps.

In John Rollin Ridge's book of Joaquin Murrieta's life published in 1854, "In The Life and Adventures of Joaquin Murrieta" he was portrayed as a folk hero who only took to a life of crime following the harshness of his life, the operation, and annihilation of everything he held dear. He was seen in the novel as a romantic and caring lover and brother who went to extremes to fight for justice for those he holds dear as well as the injustice suffered by the Mexicans.

Murrieta was respected amongst the Mexicans for his fight to defend the course of the average Mexican. Although he is seen as an outlaw, bandit, and worse, to some, he is a patriot who fought oppression and institutionalized robbery against his people. These were some of the few reasons Murrieta earned the name, Robin Hood of the West or Robin Hood of El Dorado. His life and story inspired several notable fictional books and movies. One of the most popular movies that depict the life of Murrieta was the fictional hero, "Zorro." The Mask of Zorro[10] series was released as a five-part series in 1998 and directed by Martin Campbell. In 2005 The Legend of Zorro [11]was all fallout of the life of Murrieta. His story, name, and life formed parts of the plot of both movies but told with variations to make them appealing to the audience. Other events include Johnston McCulley's "The Curse of Capistrano" that was published in 1919 by a pulp fiction magazine. "The Curse of Capistrano" was also a story about the Mexican natives of California and the operation of the downtrodden during the California Gold Rush. Don Diego Vega, in the story, always fought for the poor. His popular trademark was the mask, like the mask of Zorro. The story, therefore, still revolves around Joaquin Murrieta and the representation as a hero of the Mexican state.

For several decades, however, Joaquin Murrieta has stood as a symbol of hope and the struggle for cultural relevance in California. Murrieta represents the struggle against Anglo-American economic domination. The Association of Descendants of Joaquin Murrieta [12]defends their ancestral lineage[13] by stating that Murrieta was never a "gringo eater" but that

10.   https://www.imdb.com/title/tt0120746/

11.   https://www.imdb.com/title/tt0386140/

12.   https://opencorporates.com/companies/us_ca/C4077979

13.   https://www.ancestry.com/boards/surnames.murrieta/1.2/mb.ashx

he fought to restore the glory of Mexico and the Treaty of Guadalupe Hidalgo[14].

"The best way to find yourself is to lose yourself in the service of others."

- Mahatma Gandhi

14.   https://www.ourdocuments.gov/doc.php?flash=false&doc=26

Chapter Five: The Southern Belle

Her real name is Myra Maybelle Shirley, but popularly called the "Belle Starr" due to her legendary stance and anecdotes. Having a female outlaw for a change feels nice; therefore, we will talk about Belle Starr, who is the only female outlaw discussed in this book. However, she is also one of the few female outlaws from the Wild West. Belle Starr is also known as the Bandit Queen and ordinarily would not strike you as one who should take on the life of a bandit. She was never involved in a gunfight but was quite fond of her six-shooter.

Belle was raised in a well-to-do home and had access to proper education, which was such a rarity. There are two striking occurrences in Belle's life that could have influenced her deviation from the path created for her to one of a life of crime. Not only a life of crime but a lonely and deserted path. It is lonely and deserted not because there were very few bandits or outlaws at her time, but because there were little or no females involved in these predominantly male affairs.

So one of the critical pointers to Belle Starrs' choice of outlaws as a way of life instead of something else is her relationship with the James and Younger brothers. Yes, you read right! Belle Starr was friends with Jesse and Frank James as well as Cole Younger brothers. And, if you can recall, the James brothers are two of the most notorious bandits and outlaws of all time. Such a reputation has the potential to rub off on anyone who associates with you. A clear example is Joaquin Murrieta, whose brothers also took to a life of crime. Murrieta's nephew, Procopio, over a decade later, followed in the footsteps of his uncle. So, it does appear that negative characters or lifestyles can influence others in a negative direction too.

Early Life of Belle Starr: The Southern Belle

Belle Starr was born on February 5, 1848, in Washington County and close to Carthage, Missouri, in a log cabin. Her parents were Judge John Shirley and Elizabeth Pennington (from the Hatfield family). John was from a respectable Virginia family but was a troublesome young man. His family relocated to west-Indiana, where he met and married Elizabeth. However, John had been married and divorced twice before he met and married Elizabeth.

John and Elizabeth Shirley later relocated to Carthage, Missouri[1], and started out in agriculture, cultivating corn and wheat, as well as rearing horses and hogs. Belle Starr was the second child and first girl of five children. His brother, John Allison, was born in 1842, then came Belle in 1848 and another son, Edwin, in 1850. Two other children joined the family in later years. But that season also marked a period of boom for the Shirleys as their agriculture business experienced a steady rise.

There are two accounts as to the dates the Shirleys relocated into Carthage, Missouri. One account stated that they relocated in 1856 while another said 1860. They, however, sold off the farm before moving the family into Carthage, Missouri. When in Carthage, John Shirley purchased an inn, blacksmith shop, and a livery stable located at the Carthage town square.

When in Carthage, the family lived an enviable life. Bella Starr grew up like a queen, enjoying the good life. Compared to all the other outlaws we have discussed in this book, Belle

---

1.   https://www.legendsofamerica.com/mo-carthage/

seemed to have had a more luxurious life and was closely followed by Jesse and Frank James. Coincidentally, Belle became friends with the duo while in Missouri.

John Shirley rose within the ranks to become a respectable member of society, the seat of Carthage. His business grew to the point of taking up a long stretch of a city block. He also was the founding member of the Carthage Female Academy, where Belle Starr graduated from. Belle had an opportunity to study classical education and language in addition to learning music, with a special focus on the piano.

Her family wealth could afford her the basic necessities of life to the point she was referred to in some accounts as a spoiled brat. However, Belle Starr was a bright, polite, and talented pianist. She was also a friendly and outgoing person. One of her closest buddies was her older half-brother, John Allison, also known as Bud. Belle would often run off to the countryside in the company of her older brother. This relationship taught Belle Starr more life and survival skills than what she would learn in school. These skills were some of those she would utilize later in life, like how to ride a horse and how to shoot a gun. One lesson here is; never to pursue an education without also pursuing the skills that will help you make the best of your schooling.

Myra Belle Shirley's Life takes a U-Turn

It was in the wake of the American Civil War when the Shirleys moved into Carthage, Missouri, and the county was already getting heated. Missouri was a highly contested territory. Residents of Missouri had come to a point where they had to choose where their loyalties lie; with either the Confederates or the Union.

John Shirley and his families were Confederate supporters. During the period leading to and during the wars, you were faced with division in loyalty. One neighbor supported the Union, and the next neighbor supported the Confederates. Bud had a great influence on his younger sister to the point she unofficially worked with him in disrupting the plans of the Unionists in Missouri.

When Bud decided to become a Bushwhacker gang member, his father was proud of him. The Kansas-Missouri Border War[2] had begun, and Union and Confederate troops usually passed through the area on different missions. Union troops, popularly known as the Jayhawkers as well as the Red Legs, usually stormed different homes within the community to make an arrest or destroy communities. The Confederates and Bushwhacker supporters also launched reprisal attacks on Union supporters.

Bud was familiar with their county and therefore was a huge asset when he joined Quantrill's raiders. As a scout, he was able to point the Bushwhacker raiders in the right direction and to the right people. He was so helpful that it didn't take long before Bud was promoted to the rank of a Captain.

Things started getting too heated in Missouri. It got so complicated that Judge John's line of business suffered a major setback owing to the several raids on his business. In June 1864, things turned for the worse for the Shirley family, when the news of the murder of Bud got to the family. Bud was killed during a raid in Sarcoxie, Missouri. It threw the family into mourning. He and some other scouts had visited the home of a Confederate supporter when the unionists heard that some

Bushwhacker raiders were meeting in a home. The Union troops laid siege on the home. Immediately the Bushwhackers discovered the home had been surrounded as they tried to make an escape, but Bud was shot dead in the process.

Again, John Shirley had to sell off his businesses and properties in Missouri and relocated his family. He got a place close to Scyene, in the Southeast of Dallas, Texas.

May Belle Starr Meets Jesse and Frank James and the Cole Younger Brothers

The journey of life on the high roads and a life of crime gradually drew closer as Belle Starr met the James and Younger brother gang in Texas. In 1866, the James and Younger brothers gang just executed a successful bank robbery in Liberty, Missouri. This was their first bank robbery, and everything went according to plan, and the gang made away with $6,000 worth of cash and bonds.

To escape from the law, the gang had to split up and go on the run. Jesse and Frank James, as well as the Younger brothers, ran off to Texas. And that's where they reunited with May Belle Starr, as she provided shelter for the gang from the law. It didn't take long for Myra Shirley to become fond of Cole Younger and tactically became a member of the Jesse and Younger gang. There were speculations that Myra had an affair with Cole Younger and that her first child, Pearl, was actually his child. But Cole denied ever having any sexual relations with her, and his claim was corroborated by her brother. Cole, in his defense, said Myra was about six months pregnant when he met her again.

Myra Shirley and the gang had initially been acquaintances while growing up in Missouri. More so, her late older half-brother was in the Bushwhacker raiders with some of the gang members. Remember, he was Captain A.M. Bud of the Bushwhackers and was referred to as Captain Bud by local Confederate supporters.

However, Myra Shirley became reunited with an acquaintance of hers, known as Jim Reed. They initially met in Missouri when both Jim Reed's and Shirley's families were friends. Jim and Myra became close emotionally but lost contact after some time.

It took the Belle Starr family's relocation to Texas for her and Jim to reunite. Jim Reed needed a place to stay for the night and somehow again came in contact with the Shirleys. This reunion caused the fire between the duo to blossom again. The fire burnt so much that on November 1, 1866, they eventually got married. John and Elizabeth Shirley had no objection to her marriage since he was at that time not linked to any criminal activity.

After their marriage, Reed initially stayed with the Shirleys at Scyene, Texas. He also assisted in the farm as a way of earning an income until he got a job as a salesman in Dallas selling saddle and bridle makers. The couple later relocated to the Reed homestead in Missouri, and that's where they stayed until they started having kids.

By 1868, she had given birth to their first child and daughter named Rosie Lee, also known as Pearl. After the birth of their first child, Jim Reed took to a life of crime to make ends meet. Unfortunately, in one of his robbery operations, they shot and killed a man named Shannon in Arkansas. Therefore, the cops were after him for robbery as well as murder.

Reed knew that it was not going to be easy escaping the law if they remained in their current location, so the whole family had to relocate to California. It was when in California that they had James Edward, their second child, in 1871. Reed, however, later went back to Texas to continue his life of crime, joining a local criminal gang over there. He had initially tried his hand at farming, but I suppose the life was too slow and uneventful for him. Robbery looked more palatable and easier. He worked closely with his wife's former acquaintances like the James and the Younger brother gang. Reed also had close ties with some Native American crime gangs in the old Indian territory (now Oklahoma) who were notorious for horse rustling, cattle, and whiskey stealing.

Due to his continued brushes with the law, Reed again relocated his family to Paris, Texas. But he still did not put an end to his life of crime. In April 1874, Myra Shirley was arrested for issues related to a stagecoach robbery in Austin-San Antonio involving Reed and his gang. She was an accessory to the crime even though she didn't participate in the crime. Unfortunately, Reed did not live past August 1874, where he was shot dead during a gunfight within his gang.

Myra Shirley's Style and Personality

Myra was a smart and astute lady who grew up in a time of war and strife. Her childhood upbringing gave her all she needed to enjoy a life of glamour plus lead a decent life. But things changed too soon for Myra. However, the change did not affect her fashion sense, just as her outgoing self did not die with the situation. She was sassy and flowed well amongst the gang of outlaws.

Myra liked wearing gold earrings, a plum feathered male hat or buckskins, a black velvet gown, and moccasins. She rode sidesaddle, with two pistols and a cartridge belt saddled across her hips. She was one fine lady who knew how to pick her crowd around the list of outlaws as she commands respect in their midst. Amongst the gang and residents, Belle went by many aliases. She earned the nickname, "Bandit Queen" and "Lady Outlaw."

Myra Shirley Joins the Life of Crime

On different occasions, Myra had taken part in criminal activities. She had worked as a horse rustler, aiding robbery operations, and more, even with the James and Younger gang. In 1869, Belle Starr joined her husband and two other gang members for a robbery operation. They got a tip-off about an Old Creek Indian who has possession of about $30,000 hidden somewhere, and they wanted the cash for keeps. The gang, including Belle Starr, headed out to North Canadian River County to apprehend the man. They tortured him until he disclosed the location to pick up the gold. Belle and Jim Reed took their share of the loot and made off back to Texas.

After the death of her husband, Belle could not say no to the life crime. Therefore she dropped off her kids with her parents and headed out into the world of the outlaws. She moved into the Indian Territory (now Oklahoma) and got mixed-up with an outlaw, "Blue Duck." Blue Duck was an Indian outlaw, and his relationship did not last long as Sam Starr came into the picture, sweeping Belle off her feet.

However, there are two conflicting accounts of Belle Starr's life after the death of Reed. Apart from her closeness to Blue Duck, she was alleged to have married the uncle of Cole

Younger, Charles Younger, in 1978, but the union only lasted two weeks. To further weaken this view, Cole Younger, in his autobiography (as stated in *Belle Starr and Her Times* by Glen Shirley), denied that such an incident ever occurred.

Sam Starr was a tall, slim, fine, Cherokee gentleman. After their marriage around the mid-1870s, the lovebirds moved into Sam's luxurious property covering about sixty-two acres and located on the north of the Canadian River, close to Brairtown. It was reported that Belle Starr renamed the property, Younger's Bend, to honor her good friend, Cole Younger. However, that action sort of gives credence to the allegation of her dating the Younger gang member and possibly having a child with him. Whatever the case may be, it shows there is a kind of close affinity between Belle Starr and Cole Younger.

There was a story told by Belle Starr about a strange visitor to their home on a particular day. The slim gentleman with blinking eyes visited their home at Younger's Bend. Sam was said to feel uncomfortable about the visitor. He said the man was too calm and cold. But Myra stated that there was no cause for alarm. She then explained to Sam that the visitor is none other than her bosom friend from Missouri, blue-eyed Jesse James. A contradictory account[3] opined that Sam Starr was a long-time friend of the James and Younger brothers.

Nothing changed in the way Belle Starr lived after her marriage to Sam. The duo took to a life of crime from their base at the Canada River. Belle Starr's new union in the Indian territory gave her an opportunity to learn about horse thieving, fencing when rustling, bootleggers, planning, and organizing a suc-

---

3.   https://www.britannica.com/biography/Belle-Starr

cessful heist without being apprehended by the law. Thus began Belle Starr's life of crime fully.

Sam and Belle Starr launched out to other locations horse stealing, rustling, and bootlegging whiskey across to the Native Americans. Myra Shirley was an exceptional character. She was great at planning sting operations and getting in and out of a crime scene to minimize being caught. I suppose her years of training by her late half-brother and then from her association with James and Younger brother gang helped her with this.

The criminal couple was doing fine in their illicit business. Myra Shirley would bring her administrative skills to help organize things as well as save the gang from trouble. Belle usually pays her way out of trouble. When any member of the gang got into trouble with the law, she would dole out cash to get them free again. When things seemed to get terribly out of control, Belle Starr had her ways with the men, including using her feminine charm to soften lawmakers and enforcers in their favor. She was a great factor to their success, a person who fosters unity amongst the gang members.

Their operational base was a bit far from much attention and was located at Fort Smith, Arkansas. Judge Isaac Parker[4], the Magistrate in charge of the county, was popularly known as "the hanging Judge." The Judge was so pissed with the affairs of Belle Starr and Sam that he sought for a way to convict the couple. On several occasions, Belle Starr had been brought before his court by his Deputies. But in all instances, Belle Starr got off the hook due to a lack of evidence. She didn't get so much as a fine for bootlegging or rustling. She had at least three more

---

4.   https://www.legendsofamerica.com/ar-isaacparker/

crime-related cases, including an allegation of robbing the post office but got away, again, for lack of evidence.

Judge Parker got his chance to have a pound of flesh, but did he finally get it? Yes, he ecstatically did! Belle and Sam Starr were apprehended at Bass Reeves, trying to steal a neighbor's horse during the fall of 1882. Unfortunately, they were caught at the scene of the crime. The duo was prosecuted by U.S Prosecutor, W.H.H. Clayton, on two counts of robbery and more before they were sentenced.

Belle Starr got a light sentence - two sentences of six to nine months (another account says nine months) each to run concurrently. She was moved to the Detroit House of Corrections in Detroit, Michigan. Sam Starr was to serve one year sentence for the same crime. He was to spend his jail term in Detroit Federal Prison. One year later and both parties were back to their home at Younger's Bend. Myra Belle Starr took her jail term seriously and was of good behavior all through. She even served as an example to other inmates on how they should conduct themselves while serving a jail term. It didn't take long for her to become friends with the prison matron - her charming and outgoing nature again!

Sam, on the other hand, was the exact opposite of his wife, Belle Starr. He was so troublesome that he regularly got hard labor in jail.

If prison life had any positive impact on Sam and Belle Starr, it did not reflect one bit, as the duo were back to life as usual. It appears a life of crime was the only life they knew, even for Myra Shirley, who was born into a respectable home and had a good start in life.

Immediately after the duo settled fully from the prison experience, they were back on the streets again, rustling, bootlegging, and more. They continued unperturbed by their past experiences with the law. Belle and Sam Starr were again arrested for horse rustling and robbery barely three years after their release from jail. They were arrested by the United States marshals and taken to Fort Smith to face charges for their crimes. They again set foot into Judge Parker's court, who happily took up their case. Well, unfortunately, they got off the hook again for lack of evidence.

Belle Starr had gone in and out of jail so much and gained popularity amongst the everyday people of the county that she became more or less a celebrity. The Bandit Queen, as she was known by the locals, didn't stay out of jail for long before she appeared in a Wild West show[5] where she played the role of the female outlaw bandit. In the Wild West show, female outlaw Bella had to hold up a stagecoach in the course of a robbery operation. In another account, Richard Fox's Police Gazette made her more famous and a hero when it made reference to her as a "female Robin Hood and Jesse James." Coincidentally, she was a friend of the Jameses.

On that same year, December 17, 1886, Belle Starr received some negative news that again redefined her life. Her lover, husband, and partner in crime for over a decade, Sam Starr, was killed in a gunfight. Sam went to a friend's Christmas party and came in contact with another outlaw he had an altercation with in the past. Frank West and Sam Starr got into fresh squabbles to settle old wounds and ended up dying from their gunshot wounds inflicted on each other.

Belle really loved Sam Starr and felt her happiest moments with the love of her life just ended abruptly. But her life just kept spiraling out of control. Belle Starr was said to have gotten in and out of several relationships after the death of Sam Starr. History has it that she didn't stay so long out of marriage for the next two years. Some of the known names Belle Starr was linked with include Jim French and Jack Spaniard.

To maintain her current residence in the Indian territory, Belle Starr had to marry Jim July Starr in 1889. July was a close relative of Sam Starr and was in his mid-twenties when Belle Starr was to be about 15 years older than him.

Belle Starr's marriage to Jim July was a very rocky one. Belle seems to have a thing with bandits and outlaws as she never picks her men far from the men of the underworld. Jim July was short-tempered and threw a tantrum often. Belle had earlier caught July in an affair with a Cherokee girl, and Belle did not take it lightly. One of their numerous quarrels got Jim July so upset that he offered an acquaintance $200 to get rid of his wife. Well, his friend turned him down. This further infuriated July so much that he screamed, "Hell, I'll kill the old hag myself and spend the money for whiskey!"

I guess for Belle Starr, that day was just a normal day without much adventure or activity. Therefore, she headed out to her neighbor's house located in Eufaula, Oklahoma[6], to pay a visit. On her way back from the neighbor's home, Belle Starr took a lonely county road, riding a horse. Then suddenly, Belle Starr was ambushed by unknown assailants.

The first shot sent Belle Starr falling off her horse and to the ground. The assailant was not done with her as he came

---

6. https://en.wikipedia.org/wiki/Eufaula,_Oklahoma

closer and fired another shot to ensure that in case the first shot did not do the work, the second one will deliver the death blow. However, the report says she sustained gunshot wounds to the face, neck, shoulder, and back. That indicates the killer shot her four times. Possibly the gunshot wound to the back was the first shot that sent her falling off her horse. Afterward, other shots might have been a closer range.

Rumor has it that Belle Starr was killed using her own double-barrel gun. I really do not see how that could have happened if she was traveling with the gun and if a fight did not occur before she was shot. Perhaps more than one gun was used to kill Belle Starr. Meaning the first shot could have come from a different gun, and the killer pulls out her double-barrel gun to finish the job. Whatever the case, Myra Shirley Belle Starr died of bullet wounds at the age of 41 years and at the turn of her birthday, February 3, 1889.

There are several accounts as to what happened next after the quarrels with Jim July. One account stated that she was shot dead two days before her birthday, while another account said it was a few days after the quarrel, which would turn out to be her actual birthday.

However, Frank Eaton[7], also known as "Pistol Pete," gave an account of how Belle Starr died under different circumstances. She had come over for her usual dances. Frank stated that he was the last in the hall to dance with Belle when Edgar Watson came over to ask Belle for a dance. Watson had a few too many drinks, so he was already in a state of stupor. As expected, Belle turned his request down. This, according to Frank

---

7.   https://en.wikipedia.org/wiki/Frank_Eaton

Eaton, infuriated Edgar Watson so much he wanted to deal with Belle Starr.

After her time at the dance, Belle stepped out to go home. As she was heading home, she made a brief stop at a creek to give her horse a drink. Out of nowhere, Watson emerged and shot Belle Starr dead. In Frank's account of all that transpired, Edgar Watson was arrested, tried, sentenced, and executed (by hanging) for the murder of Myra Shirley Belle Starr. But another account said Watson was acquitted of the murder of Belle.

The story of how and who killed Belle Starr is as vast as her criminal activities were while with Sam Starr. Another account stated that due to the lack of witnesses or evidence about the murder of Belle, there were no arrests or convictions. But whatever the truth is, Belle Starr died from gunshot wounds on February 3, 1889.

Others who could be complacent (with motives) for the murder of Belle Starr included her angry and vengeful husband, Jim July, Edgar Watson, or Belle's sharecroppers[8]. The sharecroppers' link to the murder lies in the fact that he had fears Belle would turn him over to the authorities, may be to claim the ransom on his head. The sharecropper was on the run for the act of murder committed in Florida, and a reward had been placed on his head. Even some of her kids (Pearl and Eddie) were suspected of the murder of their mother. Belle lived a life that evoked so much vengeance, mistrust, and hatred that those with a motive (strong or mild) to kill her seemed many.

However, one account showed that after the death of Sam Starr, Belle wanted to take things slowly. She stopped allowing bandits to use her home as a hideout after committing crimes.

---

8.   https://en.wikipedia.org/wiki/Sharecroppers

She even refused to cover up July Jim when he got involved in horse theft.

Even after death, her anecdotes still haunted those close to her. Belle Starr's first son, Edward Reed, who already took after his mom and dad's life of crime, was arrested. Eddie had been serving as a pickup agent for criminals after they completed their raids. Later he got involved in horse theft, and in July 1889, he was arrested. Now, Judge Parker sits over the case of Eddie Reed, after trying and convicting both his mother and father of similar criminal charges several times. It will appear there is a jury-to-jail pact between the judge and the family.

Eddie was shipped to Columbus Prison, Ohio. As if that wasn't bad enough, Belle Starr's daughter, Rosie Reed, nicknamed Pearl, ended up as a prostitute just so she could raise funds for the release of her brother, Eddie Reed. Well, things were finally looking up for the family when Pearl succeeded in securing a presidential pardon for Eddie in 1893. I guess the kind gesture and possibly four years in jail caused Eddie to turn a new leaf as he chose the path of a law enforcer this time around instead of crime. Eddie became a Deputy at Fort Smith. If you remember, Fort Smith is the same location where his parents were convicted of crimes.

However, in the line of duty, Eddie killed the Crittenden brothers in 1895. So he continued until he, too, was killed on December 14, 1896, when he walked into a Saloon in Claremore, Oklahoma.

Belle Starr's corpse was laid to rest in the front of the cabin at the Younger's Bend property. All through her life and beyond, Myra Shirley, also known as Belle Starr, was loved by many and disliked by a few. From more accounts of her activities, it appears Belle Starr was involved in fewer crimes than stories and movies tend to portray. She was also said to have been more domesticated than the reports made her look. As a matter of fact, she took part in fewer robberies than she is credited with, as she stayed more at home when Sam Starr and the gang went on raids. Also, one report stated that she had left her marriage and moved in with her parents again before the death of Reeds. However, her close ties with outlaws and men involved in illicit activities made her appear more criminally inclined than in reality.

The Bandit Queen became a sensational hit in over 20 movies as her story was retold by movie makers and on television shows. Also, parts of her life and story have been a major inspiration for literary works, poems, and music for over a century now. A good example is "The Female Jesse James" by Richard K. Fox, published the year she was murdered.

Chapter Six: The Trustworthy Thief

Butch Cassidy is another interesting fellow who grew up being liked by many. Even as a youth, he was considered charming, but he, unfortunately, chose the wrong path in life. Let's discuss two events that will serve as a reminder as to how humane Cassidy could be. He should have turned out to be a fine young man, loved and respected by all, except for his criminal activities. In one instance, Cassidy forced his way into a clothing shop and stole the owner's pie and a pair of jeans. He, however, left a note promising to come back with payment for this theft. That incident turned out to be his first-ever known or recorded theft. The clothier got Cassidy arrested for theft, but he was discharged and acquitted by the trial judge.

The second event related to Cassidy's meek nature occurred in 1894 in Wyoming over issues relating to horse rustling and gang activities. One alleged incident portrayed Cassidy as a person who kept his word once he made a promise. He was standing trial for criminal activities when he pleaded with the prison guards to grant him some time off jail, promising to return the next day. Guess what? Cassidy actually came back to finish his sentence the next morning! There are other pointers we shall talk about this would-have-been fine gentleman as we go on in this chapter. If for nothing, at least he was a tall, fine, and likable gentleman.

Early Life of Butch Cassidy

Robert LeRoy Parker, popularly known as Butch Cassidy, was born April 13, 1866, exactly one year after the American Civil War. He was born in Beaver, Utah, but no one could tell for sure how his life would turn out. There are not many mentions of the life of Robert LeRoy, as much of it seemed uneventful.

Postwar America was a tough time to live for a lot of people, due to the economic downturn, high level of mistrust, plus an attempt to rebuild the economy. Butch Cassidy was the first of 13 children born to his Mormon parents from England. His parents, Maximillian Parker and Ann Campbell Gillies, got married in July 1856 before relocating to Utah later that year, and then to Circleville in 1879. At home, Cassidy was fondly called Roy. Since his parents were not very well to do, he had to carry out menial jobs to earn a living. There was no record of him having a formal education, but he took to working in western Utah as a ranch assistant. He also went over to Hay Springs, close to Milford, in search of work. It was during this time that Cassidy broke into the clothing shop to steal a pie and some jeans.

Butch Cassidy's Work-Life and Exodus to a Life of Crime

Things unexpectedly started to not look good for the Parker family in Circleville. It got worse when Maximillian Parker, Roy's dad, lost his land over property rights issues. Seeing no hope of survival in Circleville, Roy left home in his teens to begin a life of hustling. It was then he came in contact with Mike Cassidy while working at a local dairy store. Mike was a dishonest local rancher, a cattle and horse thief, and now had become friends and a mentor to Roy.

In 1884, I suppose due to the negative influence from Mike Cassidy, Roy was gradually taking to a life of crime as a cattle rustler. He stole cattle from up Parowan on the Markagunt

Plateau to sell to other buyers. It was at this point Robert LeRoy Parker changed his name to Butch Cassidy in honor of his childhood mentor, Mike Cassidy. Never underestimate the power of mentoring on one who is liberated from poverty.

At some point, he completed an apprenticeship under a butcher in Rock Springs, Wyoming. That's where Cassidy got the nickname "butcher," later shortened to "Butch," hence he became known as Butch Cassidy. In one of the accounts about Cassidy, he is painted as a Robin Hood of the Western frontier. Cassidy believed that big-time cattle ranchers were using their strength to muzzle smaller ranchers out of circulation. He then set out on the journey to the west but stopped at different locations to earn a small living on the way. Cassidy moved to Telluride County, Colorado, to the undulating foothills of Henry Mountains at Robber's Roost, and then Green River. There are speculations that he not only sought for work but possibly to trade in stolen horses.

Cassidy's next phase of life came in 1887 when he returned from Wyoming and Montana. Immediately after his return to Telluride, he met Matt Warner, a racehorse professional. That same year, Cassidy partnered with Matt Warner in horse racing at different events, and they split their earnings.

Butch Cassidy's Life of Crime

Although Cassidy had been involved in minor crimes at different stages in his life, the first notable criminal event and robbery connected to him occurred on June 24, 1889. Butch, the horse racer, Warner, as well as the McCarthy brothers stormed the San Miguel Valley Bank located in Telluride. In their first robbery[1] and one single night, the gang made away with about $21,000, which is $598,000 by today's standards.

They immediately went into hiding somewhere in the Robber's Roost. The Roost is located at Brown's Park, close to Green River, at the border of Utah and Wyoming. Once at the Vernal areas, they headed out North towards Lander, Wyoming, to stay out of track.

There were several hideouts outlaws ran to when they wanted to avoid being tracked down after a holdup. Cassidy was the first to make the run after the robbery, meandering through paths and hideouts. He headed to Mexico, going through Utah, and ended up in Montana. He found a place to hide in an area with a series of ranches and hideouts close to Monticello. This area was known as one with outlaw friendly ranch owners. Outlaws usually took on jobs there as cowboys, giving them a chance to stay away from the law. Cassidy spent about two nights at the Carlisle, near the Robber's Roost.

After the San Miguel Valley Bank robbery, Cassidy became a more notorious outlaw. If you could, however, call it a positive twist to his situation, Cassidy had his own brand as an outlaw. Based on a manuscript or memoir belonging to Roy Parker (Butch Cassidy), he was reported as fighting for the "settler's right" against long-existing cattle barons. Therefore, the bandits usually carried out small and big cattle raids and went out of circulation by hiding in the Hole-In-The-Wall. It was a natural geological and scenic formation with red sandstone escarpment located in the Old West. The area made up part of the Big Horn Mountains of Johnson County and was suitable for hideouts like the Cassidy gang. The Hole-In-The-Wall[2] is

---

1.   https://www.loc.gov/rr/news/topics/cassidy.html

now an Old Trail Town Museum in Cody, Wyoming. For these reasons, Cassidy and his gang chose it as the perfect spot to keep them safe from the law.

Well, it appears The Hole was not hidden enough, as Cassidy was arrested and sent to jail in Wyoming for some time before he regained his freedom. He returned to a life of cattle rustling.

The gang centralized their criminal activities around the Utah-Arizona border. He went a step further to put together a team of experienced and elitist outlaws and cowboys. Thus, he created the group known as the "Wild Bunch." Members of the gang include Elzy Lay, Dick Maxwell, and Harry Longabaugh, popularly known as the "Sundance Kid." Later in their series of rustling, George Currie and Henry Wilbur, a.k.a Bub Meeks, an escapee from Utah, joined the gang.

Various accounts indicated that Cassidy was never a success as a rancher. Or is there a possibility, ranching was simply a means to cover his criminal activities? Either way, Cassidy could now afford a more luxurious lifestyle. Now, he could afford a ranch of his own. In 1890, Cassidy paid in full the price for a ranch just at the border of Dubois, Wyoming. His property was well-situated across from the Hole-in-the-Wall.

Cassidy Mixes Business and Pleasure

It's not a case of all work and no play for Cassidy. Earlier in 1894, he met and fell in love with a lovely damsel known as Ann Bassett. She was a rancher and outlaw as well, as the daughter of one of Cassidy's business partners. Her father was a rancher who normally purchased fresh beef and horses from Cassidy. However, the relationship was short-lived because, in

---

2.   https://naturalatlas.com/historical-places/hole-in-the-wall-1525962

1894, the long arm of the law caught up with Cassidy at Lander, Wyoming. He was charged on counts of robbery and aiding and abetting crimes. Cassidy was known for horse rustling and possibly for aiding the escape of other outlaws.

Butch Cassidy was sentenced to two years imprisonment at the Wyoming State prison in Laramie, Wyoming. I guess he had luck on his side, as Cassidy only served 18 months out of the two-year term. Governor William Alford Richards[3] granted him pardon after he was released from jail in January 1896. Cassidy had a brief affair with Ann Bassett's older sister and, for some reason, came back to dating Ann Bassett. There wasn't much to link Ann directly to any of the Wild Bunch's criminal activities.

Butch Cassidy's Wild Bunch Goes Fully Operational

It appears the Wild Bunch took some time to get a sense of direction and get things going. Prior to 1896, Cassidy had a random association of bandits he used for robbery operations or horse rustling. At this point, the innocent little boy from Utah was gone and in his place was an outlaw and rogue. Thus, the Wild Bunch was born. Other members of the gang include Laura Bullion, Will News Carver, Ben Kilpatrick, Harvey Kid Curry, Harry Tracy, and George Flat Nose Curry. The name of the gang was a motivation from Doolin-Dalton's[4] gang of outlaws, also known as the Wild Bunch. So, the spate of robbery began.

Cassidy, Logan, Bob Meeks, and Lay executed a heist at the Montpelier bank in Idaho on August 13, 1896. The group

---

3.   https://history.nebraska.gov/collections/william-alford-richards-1849-1912-rg0720am

4.   https://www.usmarshals.gov/history/dalton/doolin-dalton.htm

made away with about $7,000. It was after this robbery that Harry Alonzo Longabaugh joined the Wild Bunch. Harry Alonzo, a.ka. The Sundance Kid, was a notorious outlaw who drove the stakes higher for the Wild Bunch.

The Wild Bunch had to retreat to the Robbers Roost in 1897 to plan their next robbery in early April. This time the gang chose to operate within their locality. There was a small group of staff from the Pleasant Valley Coal Company moving valuables or funds for payroll on April 22, 1897. As the men approached the mining town of Castle of Gate in Utah, the Wild Bunch laid an ambush and carted away $7,000 in gold.

It was one robbery to another, as there was no stopping the Wild Bunch anymore. After each successful raid, the group retreated to the Robbers Roost to lay low for a few weeks before launching another attack.

Barely three months after the Pleasant Valley Coal Company robbery, the gang struck again on June 2, 1899. But this time it was a passenger train belonging to the Union Pacific Overland Flyer[5] at Wilcox, Wyoming. The Wilcox, Wyoming incident increased the popularity of the Wild Bunch, but it also brought them closer to the eyes of the law enforcement agents. Security operatives got on the trail of the Wild Bunch, but fortunately, they seemed above the reach of the law. George and Kid Curry went all out and engaged in a shootout with the law. They even scored a point against the law enforcement agents when they shot and killed Sheriff Joe Hazen in the course of the shootout.

The whole affair did not go down well with the government. Therefore, the Pinkerton National Detective Agency

(PNDA) was contracted to find the bandits. PNDA was the same agency that attempted to track down Jesse and Frank James for their train robbery in Gads Hill, Missouri, in the 1860s. A team of crack detectives from the agency was placed on the manhunt. Killer-for-hire detective, Tom Horn, explosive expert, Bill Speck, and detective Charles Siringo were all part of the team. However, Detective Charles was commissioned to hunt down the Wild Bunch after he had been briefed about the killing of Sheriff Hazen during the shootout.

Detective Charles, through investigation, became friends with one Elfie Landusky. Elfie had a child with Kid Curry's younger brother, Lonny. And he hoped that he could glean useful information to help him apprehend the group.

One month after the train robbery, Lay and the gang members struck again on July 11, 1899. This time, they ambushed the Colorado and Southern Railroad [6]train close to Folsom, New Mexico[7]. Well, unfortunately, they never expected the welcome that greeted them. Immediately the ambush was in progress; law enforcement officers from the county opened fire on the gang. In the ensuing gunbattle, Lay shot Sheriff Henry Love and Edward Farr dead. As always, the gang split up after a robbery and regrouped at the designated spot, either in Fannie Porter's brothel, located at San Antonio, Texas, or Hole-in-the-Wall at the Robbers Roost.

When Lay was finally arrested, he was charged on two counts of robbery and murder. The jury sentenced Lay to life imprisonment to be spent at the New Mexico State Penitentiary.

---

6.   https://en.wikipedia.org/wiki/Colorado_and_Southern_Railroad

7.   https://en.wikipedia.org/wiki/Folsom,_New_Mexico

The Wild Bunch had gone really wild, and Cassidy seemed to be a master strategist, planning their heists and creating routes for their escape. They became invisible, almost always evading the law. Their train and bank robberies continued across New Mexico, Nevada, South Dakota, and Wyoming. As the list of robberies kept increasing, so did the amount realized for a single robbery vary. On one occasion, the Wild Bunch ambushed a train near Folsom, New Mexico, and got away with $70,000, nearly 2 million dollars in 2019 standards.

However, the irony of this was that the Wild Bunch became a sensational story in the eyes of the public. Their anecdotes were like a movie, for some segments of the audience yearned for more escapades about Cassidy, the Sundance Kid, and the other gang members.

Cassidy Almost Gets an Amnesty

In 1900, an amnesty arrangement was worked out for Cassidy just to put an end to his robbery activities. There are two accounts on the issue of an amnesty for Butch Cassidy. One account indicated that the arrangement was initiated between Governor Heber Wells of Utah and the Union Pacific Railroad. The company proposed to drop the charges against Cassidy for the recent robbery on the company's train. The company's chairman, E.H. Harriman, was willing to discuss terms with Cassidy through Matt Warner. The Wild Bunch had become so notorious that the Union Pacific Railroad was willing to sign a pact with Cassidy. They also offered him a job as security personnel if he would accept, but Cassidy surprisingly turned down the offer.

However, another account stated that Cassidy approached Governor Wells to grant him amnesty in exchange for putting an end to his robbery activities.

The second account stated that the amnesty came as a proposition from Cassidy to the Union with the cooperation of Governor Wells.

However, on August 29, 1900, they broke the pact. Cassidy violated the terms of the amnesty when he, the Sundance Kid, and others raided the Union's train again in Tipton, Wyoming.

Butch Cassidy's Death and the Surrounding Controversy

The Union Pacific Railroad's business felt threatened by the Wild Bunch gang. Since the pact did not work out, they desperately needed another solution, and fast. Therefore, they contracted the Pinkerton Detectives to get the job done.

By now, you should have come to realize that the Pinkerton detectives' ability to deal with such cases precedes the group. They didn't waste much time to get on the hunt for Cassidy, the Sundance Kid, and the others. Well, their presence did not deter the Wild Bunch gang, but they did eventually disperse to South America. One account, therefore, indicated that the Cassidy and Sundance Kid lost their lives in a shootout with soldiers during a robbery on November 6, 1908, in Southern Bolivia.

The truth about how Cassidy and the rest of the gang died is still unclear, as there are different accounts on how they died or what caused their death. Some reports state that Cassidy escaped unhurt, faked his death, and only went into hiding. Some years later, he returned to the United States under the name of William T. Phillips. Williams spent the remaining three decades of his life working as a machinist. He finally died from cancer in Spokane, Washington in 1937. Parts of what fueled the assumption about the link between Cassidy and William Phillips was his book written in 1920, known as "[8]Bandit Invincible: The Story of Butch Cassidy[9]." The in-depth account of the life of Butch Cassidy told by Phillips in his book made it clear that this could only come from the author's personal experience.

In John Mcphee's book "Annals of the Former World[10]," he gave an account of Cassidy's last few days. It was an account given to Dr. Francis Smith by David Love in the 1930s. It stated that Cassidy went to Paris for facial surgery. Cassidy then gave Dr. Smith proof by showing him a bullet wound treated by the doctor several years back.

In Josie Bassett's account given in 1960, Cassidy might have died in Jonnie, Nevada, about 15 years earlier. He had paid her a visit in 1920 after his return from South America. Circleville, Utah residents[11], also had their own version. They claimed that Cassidy lived and worked in their midst in Nevada until his dying days.

Going by some of those accounts, it would be tempting to assume Butch Cassidy survived the gunbattle with the soldiers in Bolivia. However, the fact still remains that his days as an outlaw officially came to an end there, until he eventually died.

8.   http://www.nbcnews.com/id/44146181/ns/us_news-life/t/did-butch-cassidy-survive-ripe-old-age/#.Xra1o2hKiM8

9.   http://www.nbcnews.com/id/44146181/ns/us_news-life/t/did-butch-cassidy-survive-ripe-old-age/#.Xra1o2hKiM8

10.   https://www.pulitzer.org/winners/john-mcphee

11.   https://utah.com/old-west/butch-cassidy

Though Butch Cassidy's[12] final days remain an unsolved puzzle, he made a considerable impact as a Wild West Outlaw. His anecdotes gave birth to several literary works and movies like the 1969 Oscar award-winning movie, Butch Cassidy and the Sundance Kid[13] with Paul Newman acting as Cassidy and Robert Redford as Sundance.

12.   https://www.biography.com/crime-figure/butch-cassidy

13.   https://time.com/5682980/butch-cassidy-sundance-kid-history/

Chapter Seven: Four's the Charm

What makes the outlaws in this chapter more intriguing is due to their antecedents. Of all outlaws discussed so far in this book, this set of outlaws present unique traits worth noting. Three siblings, four outlaws, two law enforcement officers turned outlaws, two simultaneous bank robberies on the same day, and the shortest-surviving robbery gang or outlaws (two and a half years) we have discussed - all this is what makes the Dalton Brothers tale a must-read.

This is the story of four of America's most notorious outlaws - bank and train robbers in the Wild West. The siblings and gang members are Gratton Hanley "Grat" Dalton born on March 30, 1861, in Lawrence, Kansas, William Marion "Bill" Dalton was born in 1863 in Cass County, Missouri, Robert Rennick "Bob" Dalton was born on May 13, 1869, in Cass County, Missouri, and Emmett Dalton; born May 3, 1871, in Belton, Missouri.

The boys all started out as enterprising young men, looking for a source of livelihood. Like every other young man, they had their own shortcomings and negative habits, but nothing unusual, at least at first. The boys even took sides with the law, by becoming U.S. Deputies. But soon enough, things got out of control.

The End

Bob Dalton was a skilled and daring young man. He said he wanted to "beat anything Jesse James ever did - rob two banks at once, in broad daylight."

The plan was all laid out! There was no room for failure; everything was set. And on October 5, 1892, Bob and his Dalton gang[1] set out on one of the wildest bank robberies of all time[2] - two robberies in one swoop! The location? Coffeyville[3], Kansas. Bob and Emmett were scheduled to rob the First National Bank, and Grat, Broadwell, and Power will invade the Condon Bank just across the road. Emmett was skeptical about the whole operation. He didn't want anyone from the area injured or to recognize him, since he attended Robbin's Corners, and the boys had lived in the area before. He was popular among the residents of Coffeyville. But Bob saw things differently.

From the onset, there were some technical flaws with their operational plan. Although Emmett saw it and protested, Bob wouldn't listen, maybe because he had a death wish. The gang arrived at Coffeyville early to execute their plan when the first error played out. They had planned to tie their horses on a post directly behind Condon Bank to avoid attracting attention. But because they failed to do an earlier assessment of the operation area before that day, the gang did not realize that the post was no longer there, but had been removed during reconstruction work.

Bob suggested a new location at an alley, adjacent to the Condon Bank and close to the City jail. The new location, now called Dalton's Alley, only helped to compromise their covert operations. As the bandits walked out of the alley, heading to

---

1.   https://www.legendsofamerica.com/we-dalton/

2.   https://www.history.com/this-day-in-history/the-dalton-gang-is-wiped-out-in-coffeyville-kansas

3.   https://www.britannica.com/place/Coffeyville

the banks, a storekeeper sweeping the sidewalk spotted them. Their mustaches and disguises called attention to them. The storekeeper immediately ran into his store to try to avoid any confrontation. As the gang exited the alley into Walnut Street with their Winchester rifles tucked around their legs, Emmet and Bob crossed into Union Street and into the First National Bank. Broadwell, Grat, and Powers rushed into the Condon Bank but not until they had been spotted by one of those carrying out street work. The gentleman called out to others, "The Daltons are robbing the bank!"

The street workers screamed and alerted other businessmen in the area, but it did not deter the Dalton gang from their operation. Grat went straight to the cashier once within the banking hall of the Condon Bank. Pointing his Winchester gun at the cashier, Grat gave him a sack bag and told him to fill the sack with cash. Broadwell and Power stood by the entrance to avert any external attack. Grat went over the manager's office and ordered him to come to the front office. Next, Grat ordered them to open the vault so they could make away with some gold and valuables. But the manager explained that the vault uses a timer and would only open after ten minutes before inputting the passcode.

At the First National Bank, Bob and Emmett had already gotten the bank officials, two customers, and cashier to cooperate. They requested the cashier, Thomas Ayers, to open the safe, placed the gold and cash into their sacks, and were ready to leave. Immediately they seized Ayers to use as a human shield as they prepared to go outside through the front door.

If you remember, on September 7, 1876, the James and Younger brother gang attacked the First National Bank of

Northfield, Minnesota, while the Dalton gang chose the Coffeyville Bank, Kansas.

Bob and Emmett planned on dashing out to join Grat and the others at Condon Bank. Afterward, the whole gang planned to head for the alley, get their horses, and then be on the run. Unfortunately, the men of the town already had a different plan and surprise waiting for them outside.

When the duo came out through the front door of the First National Bank, an American Express personnel stationed outside opened fire on them. Bob and Emmett responded from their Winchester guns and immediately ran back into the banking hall. They made a quick run for the rear door, still carrying the sack of cash and intending to effect their escape plan. This time, Emmet and Bob took two bank employees as human shields.

Meanwhile, in Condon Bank, Grat heard the gunshot from the American Express agent and realized that he might not be able to escape with such a heavy sack of money and silver. Therefore, Grat requested they remove silver while stashing as much cash as their pockets could carry.

On the streets, a hardware store around the corner had started giving out guns to the locals standing around. The locals then took strategic positions, facing the Condone Bank, and began firing into the bank through the windows. Grat, Power, and the Broadwells returned fire while waiting for the vault timer to go on so they could carry more cash. Their shots hit and injured some of the locals.

Emmet and Bob emerged from the rear of the First National Bank and came face to face with Lucius Baldwin, who had been positioned there with his pistol facing the rear door. Bob ordered Lucius to drop his weapon, but he wouldn't budge. So Bob took him out with one shot. They ran towards the alley and turned onto Eighth Street, headed towards Condone Bank. What they saw hit them like a storm! A couple of town folks were shooting into the Condone Bank, George Cubine from the drug store on the axis of First National Bank was positioned in front of the bank, waiting for Bob and Emmet in case they came out through the front again. Bob immediately shot him dead with one bullet to the head. Once Charles Brown, Cubine's partner, saw that his partner had been hit, he quickly bent to pick up his rifle since he had no ammunition. He lifted the rifle towards Bob, but was killed by him instead.

When Thomas Ayers of First National saw that Bob and Emmet ran off, leaving him unharmed, he quickly dashed into the hardware store to get a rifle. As Bob turned around from his confrontation with Brown, he raised his head to see Ayers about two hundred feet away, raising a rifle at him. He didn't waste a second more and shot Ayers. The bullet delivered a deadly blow on Ayers, strong enough to leave him paralyzed for the rest of his life.

It was a showdown, a historical moment, and a day to remember for decades to come: gunfire and bullets were flying everywhere, but more to the Condone Bank. In the crossfire, Powers got hit on the arm. To effect their escape, Grat took the staff of the bank into the bank office and made them lay down. With the signal from Bob, the trio exited through the side door, ducking and crouching as they ran. They turned to the side and ran into Walnut Street to get their horses. The five of them reunited at the alley, carrying their sacks of money.

As the Dalton gang mounted their horses and turned east towards the horse's town, Marshal Charles T. Connelly came into the livery stable but didn't notice the gang. He ran westward, heading to the plaza in search of the bandits. Grat turned right in time to see Connelly heading west and immediately shot him in the head, killing him on the spot. Marshal John Kholer was still within the stable but right behind the track of Connelly. Noticing Connelly drop dead, he raised his pistol almost at the same time as Grat, who was turning on him too. Before Grat could take a shot, Kholer pulled the trigger, hitting Grat in the throat.

As Bob focused on getting the team out of the area, he took a fatal hit to the head and heart from shooters at the hardware store. Bob Dalton, the leader of the Dalton gang, died on the spot. Power immediately mounted his horse but received a torrent of gunfire and dropped to the ground, dead. Emmet mounted his horse successfully and made a quick escape unhurt. But he turned in time to see Bob hit by a busload of bullets. He couldn't leave his friend hanging, so he made a u-turn (a costly mistake) to go rescue him by carrying him on his horse. Emmet instead received a downpour of bullets and fell to the ground. Broadwell was hit at several spots but was still able to make an escape. He, however, dropped dead about two miles away from the crime scene.

The robbery stint was taking longer than Bill Dalton and Bill Doolin[4] had expected. Their roles involved waiting for the five gang members to return from the raid while they provided extra horses as means of escape. With the five nowhere in sight,

---

4.   https://www.britannica.com/biography/Bill-Doolin

they got fed up with waiting, only to hear about the failed robbery attempt.

The whole robbery started by 9:30 in the morning, the gunfight afterward lasted 15 minutes, and in a single moment, the lives of four able-bodied young men with such youthful zest and intelligence were laid to waste due to their choices in life. Three outlaws were killed on the spot, one ran off but died later, another captured and survived, two never came close to the robbery scene.

Emmet Dalton got a second chance in life as he survived the ordeal but was captured by security forces. He sustained serious bullet wounds to the right arm, shoulder, hip, and groin. About 18 bullets found their way to his back with another 7 hitting other parts of his body. Emmet was sent to recover at the Kansas State Penitentiary[5] located at Lansing, Kansas. He was supposed to spend the rest of his life in jail but got off with a pardon after serving about 14 years. Clearly, Emmett Dalton had more working for him, unlike the other Dalton gang members. He lived another 45 years after the failed robbery incident and moved to Hollywood, California, to work as a real estate agent, an actor, and author. Thus, Emmet died at age 66 in 1937. Emmett said the motivation to continue in a life of robbery was the continued chase from Deputy US Marshal Heck Thomas. The gang wanted to execute a big raid, robbing the banks and then moving out of the territory. They thought of a fresh start without having Thomas on their back anymore. But I guess they never lived to see that day.

The two Dalton gang members who were never at the scene of the robbery were Charles Pierce and Bill Doolin - "Bitter

---

5.   https://en.wikipedia.org/wiki/Kansas_State_Penitentiary

Creek" Newcomb. Well, the duo never had first-hand experience of how the whole event of October 5, 1892, played out, so I suppose they did not learn a lesson. Bill Dalton set out a spate of robberies and later formed the Doolin-Dalton Gang.

There were several suspected robbery incidents linked to the Doolin-Dalton Gang for the next few years. On September 1, 1893, there was a gun battle that resulted in the death of three Deputy US Marshal in Ingalls, Oklahoma. Bill's gang was also suspected for the robbery of May 21, 1894, at First National Bank in Longview, Texas.

Finally, it was Bill's turn to experience a painful death. On June 8, 1894, while Bill thought he had a right to enjoy a peaceful life, he was at the front porch of his farmhouse playing with his daughter. Well, the law enforcement felt it was time to say leave without even a goodbye to his family. The lawmen snuck behind him at the Ardmore farmhouse and shot Bill Dalton dead. Nine deputy US Marshals and one outlaw.

However, in a related twist, the nine Deputy US Marshals faced murder charges over the killing of Bill Dalton. After the federal court hearing at Ardmore, no single marshal was indicted, which makes it all the more puzzling what actually happened during the robbery, Bill's murder, and the trial of the marshals.

In the early 1890s, Bill Dalton had settled into a normal and respectable life. He got married and started having kids. Bill also ventured into politics as a member of the Populist Party. In the course of his activities, Bill got into the Populist fight, pitching him against the Railroad candidate. The issue had to do with the land disputes with the Southern Pacific Railroad company versus the local farmers, and Bill was on the side of the locals.

How it All Began

Lewis Dalton was the father of three of the Dalton gang members. He was born in Kentucky and lived there for some years before relocating to Missouri. He started out as a saloon keeper and rambler once in Kansas City, Kansas, and got married to Adeline Lee Younger. This means the Dalton brothers[6] were relatives of the Younger brothers of the James and Younger gang.

The couple gave birth to fifteen kids in total, but lost two in their infancy. With the families relocation to Coffeyville, Kansas, they became exposed to so much violence. They annexed the Missouri-Kansas border, witnessed the effect of the American Civil War and the Quantrill Raider as well as other guerilla groups. The family, at some point, lived in the Oklahoma Indian Territory[7]. At some point, Lewis Dalton left home for an undisclosed reason, leaving Adeline to care for their fifteen kids.

Bob, Emmett, Grat, and Littleton were cowboys until 1887, when they began assisting their older brother, Frank Dalton, in fighting crime.

The Daltons Becomes US Marshals

Frank Dalton became a Deputy US Marshal attached to the federal court in Fort Smith, Arkansas. He, however, was shot dead by whiskey runners on November 27, 1887, in the line of duty. The event occurred as a result of a gunbattle with

---

6.   https://www.britannica.com/topic/Dalton-Brothers

7.   https://www.britannica.com/place/Oklahoma-state

the Smith-Dixon Gang. Bob Dalton had already joined the force before Frank's death as he worked under Frank.

Bob and Grat Dalton continued as US Marshalls in Fort Smith, Arkansas, and Bob introduced Emmet into the force by giving him the responsibility of guarding prisoners. Bob got more responsibilities when he was assigned to organize the police force at the Osage Nation post. He always moved with Emmet Smith as his deputy to his new duty post.

An account indicated that things went rough for Bob and Emmett when they didn't get any payment for a period. Therefore, in 1889, the duo took to horse stealing as a way to survive. They carried their operations out even with their police badges still on. They were kicked out of the force about a year after the incident.

Birth of the Dalton Gang

Horse thievery looked more rewarding than working for the law, so the duo went into a life of crime full-time. Well, the laws weren't going to allow them to get away with their crime in Kingfisher, Oklahoma, but the duo escaped leaving Grat Dalton to bear the brunt. Grat spent two weeks in jail while Bob and Emmett ran off to California to work for their older brother, Bill, on his ranch. Bill Dalton had a ranch close to San Miguel in San Luis Obispo County, California.

The duo continued the life of horse thievery for some year while Bob Dalton had something bigger, more adventurous, but more dangerous in mind - rob a train! Emmett, Bill, and Littleton were totally against Bob's train robbery idea.

Emmett later went with Bob on the robbery on February 6, 1891, just as a spectator. They finally robbed the Southern Pacific Railroad passenger train close to Alila successfully. So, the motivation to continue robbery was born.

March 17, 1891, Bill Dalton, Bob Emmett, and Grat were charged for the Alila robbery at the Tulare County Grand Jury. Bill and Grat were then locked in the Tulare County jail while Bob and Emmet were declared wanted with a $3,000 reward on the heads.

Bob and Emmet escaped to Oklahoma and went out of circulation. However, this was not without the help of big brother Bill Dalton who arranged their escape long before he was arrested. Bill always had their back, shielding them from the arm of the law, planning and executing their escape. Sheriff Kay had a difficult time tracking down Emmet and Bob and therefore gave up the chase.

Bob and Emmett, thrilled by their success and escape, they went ahead to institute the Dalton Gang.

Lesson:

Never allow temporary setbacks and disappointments to stop you from trying or taking the next big step in life.

During the robbery at Alila, a fireman working on the train was hit by a bullet. Grat Dalton was therefore charged for murder. His trial was manipulated even though he had an alibi, which showed he truly was in Fresno, California, when the robbery occurred. The Southern Pacific Railroad wanted Grat punished for the crime of his brothers due to the death of the fireman. But the fireman was accidentally shot by the express-man and not Bob or Emmett.

Grat got a life sentence, but with external help and the support of big brother Bill, he and two other prisoners escaped on September 20, 1891. Someone slipped a saw into the prison to aid their escape from the Tulare County Prison in Visalia. But Bill stayed behind in his cell playing a famous song, "You'll Never Miss My Brother Till He's Gone" on his guitar. But he was eventually released on October 15 for lack of evidence against him.

The other two escapees were arrested by Sheriff Kay, leaving Grat Dalton. Kay, based on a tip-off, tracked Grat to California. Riley Dean helped Grat escape, and there were supposed to be at the hideout somewhere in the summit of a mountain located near the Kings River and close to Sanger, California.

On December 24, 1891, Sherif Kay, representing Tulare County and Sheriff Hensley, representing Fresno County, got on the hunt. They climbed the mountain towards their hiding place and in search of Grat. Later on, that same location became known as the Daltons camp.

Grat got a heads up and was able to make an escape before Kay got to him. He had to shoot at Sheriff Kay and Hensley to make the escape, but Riley Dean was not that successful. He was arrested while Grat went to a friend's house in Livingston, California. Brother Cole Dalton then helped Grat continue his escape to Oklahoma.

Finally, it was time to put the Dalton Gang into full force - robbing trains and banks. Grat came back to Oklahoma during the Spring of 1892. Bill Dalton had earlier moved into his mother's place, close to Kingfisher after his release from jail. Emmett, Robert Rennick, and Bob Dalton all returned to California, and they began the plan. The Dalton Gang was born, and Bill Dalton helped to make their escape possible, offered to advise, and served as a spy.

The Dalton Gang continued their life of crime until everything came crumbling down on October 5, 1891, in the twin robbery incident. Although they died as criminals, their story became a source of inspiration, movies, and other literary works for decades to come.

Final Words

Many legendary outlaws died young - Billy the Kid died at 21 years, Jesse James died at age 34, Joaquin Murrieta died at age 23, Myra Shirley - Belle Star died at 41; all in their prime.

Emmet was involved in his last robbery at the age of 21 and died at 66, Bob was 23, Grat was 31, and Bill 25; all part of America's history. This crew of legendary outlaws had the potential to make America proud. If the narratives of their lives were different, they could have become some of America's greatest inventors, broadcasters, industrialists, entertainers, clergy, or more. But their experiences, life, and times defined their outcomes.

There is no gain saying that the outlaws of the West provided an exciting reading. But there is more to learn from their story by taking a look at their life and times. Most of the outlaws of the West were a product of their time - events surrounding the American Civil War, the great recession, and the building of a state where each person can enjoy the liberty to live their dreams.

"I am convinced that life is 10% what happens to me and 90% how I react to it. And so it is with you... we are in charge of our attitudes." - **Charles R. Swindoll**

If we all use our circumstances and situations as excuses for leading questionable lives, then there would hardly be anyone free from a life of crime, or at least getting away with some misdeeds.

Some of the outlaws had a good start but allowed negative influences to define who they became. Mentoring, negative programming, and leadership can redefine a person's existence. People lead for different reasons, and the type of leadership you get or subscribe to will determine the outcomes of your life. But I also give some credit to most of the outlaws we have discussed. They were mostly die-hard believers in their abilities.

"If you believe you can, you probably can. If you believe you won't, you most assuredly won't." - **Denis Waitley**

Another perk in favor of the outlaws of the Wild West was their ability to take action and not procrastinate about their dreams, aspirations, and pursuits in life.

"Do you want to know who you are? Don't ask. Act! Action will delineate and define you." - **Thomas Jefferson**

Did you also notice that some of the outlaws were great strategic planners, focused achievers, and team players? At least for as long as the game lasted, they did well. Bob Dalton, Myra Shirley, Butch Cassidy, Billy the Kid, Jesse and Frank James, were all good planners and actionable people - not dreamers.

"Our goals can only be reached through a vehicle of a plan, in which we must fervently believe, and upon which we must vigorously act. There is no other route to success."

- Pablo Picasso

There will always be the downtrodden in society, and some people must rise up in their defense. You could be the next Murrieta Jaoquin defending the course of others - but not through the wrong means.

Another thing to note about these outlaws is their team spirit. When Frank James left the scene, Jesse James' operations and the team were no longer as smooth as they could have been. Teamwork and having the right people on a team will determine how far you can rise. If you ask me, I think Frank was the brains, and Jesse was the striking force of the Jesse James gang. The last point is; most of the outlaws provided excellent social support systems for others, standing up for their friends, and being their brother's keeper. Family and the support of friends are essential tools for survival and finding your spark in life.

"Life consists not in holding good cards but in playing those you hold well."

- John Billings

We all are products of not only our environment but our decisions in life. We started this book with a promise to deliver value for your time, and you would agree you got great value from this book. This is not only a compendium of America's Wild West history from the 18th and 19th centuries, but it is also an interesting read, more like a bedtime story using real and factual life experiences to entertain, inspire change, and aid your development. All details contained in this book have been thoroughly researched to help you appreciate past history, avoid future mistakes, and make better decisions in life.

It was great having you on a ride through the West. If you find this book as exciting as it was for me to research and put it together, please leave a comment and review. I wish you an eventful time going down memory lane.

Don't miss out!

Visit the website below and you can sign up to receive emails whenever Daniel Brand publishes a new book. There's no charge and no obligation.

https://books2read.com/r/B-A-YKHF-ZVUHB

BOOKS 2 READ

Connecting independent readers to independent writers.

Did you love *Outlaws of the Wild West: Infamous Western Criminals and Killers*? Then you should read *The Irishman, Gotti, and Mafia Hitmen: The Organized Crime Bundle*[1] by Daniel Brand!

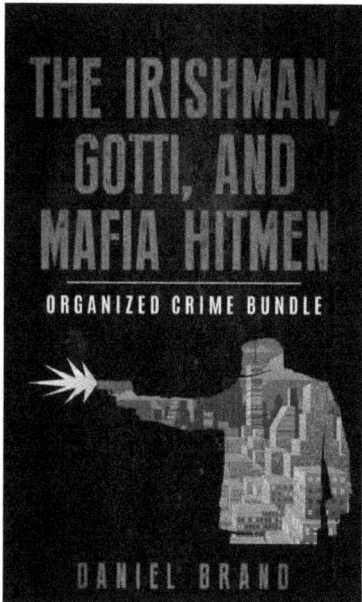

Frank Sheeran, known as **the Irishman**, waited his entire life to tell his story, or at least his version of his story. The world knew him as a union official, a long-time member of the Teamsters Union; he was a member of Jimmy Hoffa's inner circle at the top of the national union. He had run-ins with the law in this position. He was charged with the murder of a rebel union member in a riot that occurred outside the Teamster's Local

---

1. https://books2read.com/u/49QwdW

2. https://books2read.com/u/49QwdW

Philadelphia Union Hall, but the charges were later dropped. He went to prison in the 80s after being caught on a wire instructing once of his crew to break someone's legs and was named in Rudy Giuliani's Mafia Commission Trial as an unindicted co-conspirator and one of only two non-Italian members of the Mafia Commission.

As an old man suffering from cancer that would soon kill him, Frank Sheeran shared his story with his attorney. He told him of the things that were already known, but he shared much, much more. This book explores Frank Sheeran's confessions as a lifelong criminal with ties to <u>some of the biggest crimes of the 20th century.</u>

This book also comes with the books. **<u>Gotti,</u> and <u>Mafia Hitmen and Assassins</u> as a <u>BONUS</u>.**

Inside this book, you will find:

A detailed account of Frank Sheeran's time in the army during the second world war, where he was in combat for an astounding four hundred and eleven days, with a focus on the war crimes he has admitted to;

A look into Sheeran's post-war slides into a life of crime, finding himself working for the Mafia before he even knew what the Mafia was;

Information on his time as a hitman for the Mafia and how that led him to work for Jimmy Hoffa as muscle and hitman for the powerful Teamster Boss;

Frank Sheeran's accounts of his connections to the Bay of Pigs Invasion and the Assassination of JFK; and

His confession to the murders of Crazy Joe Gallo and of his friend, Jimmy Hoffa.

Also by Daniel Brand

9 781733 755054